The Ethics of Metropolitan Growth

Think Now

Think Now is a brand-new series of stimulating and accessible books examining key contemporary social issues from a philosophical perspective. Written by experts in philosophy, these books offer sophisticated and provocative yet engaging writing on political and cultural themes of genuine concern to the educated reader.

Available now:

The Ethics of Climate Change, James Garvey
War and Ethics, Nicholas Fotion
Terrorism, Nicholas Fotion, Boris Kashnikov and Joanne K. Lekea
Personal Responsibility, Alexander Brown
Nanoethics, Dónal P. O'Mathúna

Forthcoming:

Beyond Animal Rights, Tony Milligan
Digital Justice, Justine Johnstone
Identity Crisis, Jeremy Stangroom
Just Warriors, Inc., Deane-Peter Baker
The Ethics of Trade and Aid, Christopher D. Wraight

Series Editors:
James Garvey is Secretary of The Royal Institute of Philosophy and author of *The Twenty Greatest Philosophy Books* (Continuum)
Jeremy Stangroom is co-editor, with Julian Baggini, of *The Philosophers' Magazine* and co-author of *Why Truth Matters, What Philosophers Think* and *Great Thinkers A–Z* (all Continuum).

The Ethics of Metropolitan Growth

The Future of our Built Environment

Robert Kirkman

continuum

Continuum International Publishing Group
The Tower Building   80 Maiden Lane
11 York Road   Suite 704
London   New York
SE1 7NX   NY 10038

www.continuumbooks.com

© Robert Kirkman, 2010

British Library Cataloguing-in-Publication Data
A catalogue record for this book is available from the British Library.

ISBN: HB: 978-1-4411-1312-2
        PB: 978-1-4411-0280-5

Library of Congress Cataloging-in-Publication Data
Kirkman, Robert, 1968-
  The ethics of metropolitan growth : the future of our built environment / Robert
Kirkman.
     p. cm.
  Includes bibliographical references.
  ISBN-13: 978-1-4411-1312-2 (HB)
  ISBN-10: 1-4411-1312-6 (HB)
  ISBN-13: 978-1-4411-0280-5 (pbk.)
  ISBN-10: 1-4411-0280-9 (pbk.)
  1. Cities and towns—Growth—Moral and ethical aspects. 2. Urbanization—Moral and
ethical aspects. 3. City planning—Moral and ethical aspects. I. Title.

  HT371.K49 2010
  174'.93071216--dc22

                                                                        2009019739

Typeset by Servis Filmsetting Ltd, Stockport, Cheshire

Printed and bound in Great Britain by the MPG Books Group

for Corwyn and Dorothea

Contents

Preface

I grew up in the suburbs. To be specific, from the time I was two until I left for college at seventeen, my family lived in a two-story, single-family home in a subdivision that was built in the 1960s on what had been farmland near Toledo, Ohio. We had a two-car garage and a hedge in the front, and a patio, barbecue grill, and above-ground swimming pool in the back.

In many ways, my experiences growing up were typical of white, middle-class American children of my generation, a generation that came on the scene when the suburbanization of the United States was already well under way. I walked and biked around the neighborhood, and played with or avoided the children of other white, middle-class families. I went to the mall on weekends with family or with friends, often simply to pass the time – though I was unusually fond of passing time in bookstores. I watched too much television.

I also witnessed the process of suburbanization itself, though I cannot claim to have understood it at the time. Some years ago, I had the chance to look at a series of aerial photographs of the area where I grew up, taken at intervals from 1939 to 1998. As I looked at them, early memories of home came into focus and took on new meaning.

In the first photograph there are only the county fairgrounds surrounded by a grid of perfectly square farm fields cut diagonally by a railroad line. In the photo from the 1950s, the Ohio Turnpike slices across the landscape and the first few developments appear.

In the photo from the late 1960s, more developments are in place and my childhood home is under construction.

What struck me most about that particular image is that my old neighborhood, which for a long time seemed to me the very center of civilization, was in fact perched on the outer edge of development: had it occurred to me to do so as a child, I could have walked to the end of my block, climbed over two fences, and set out across open fields to the far horizon. By the mid 1970s, there was already another layer of subdivisions in place, a buffer between my neighborhood and open country. By the late 1990s several layers of commercial development and industrial parks had been added, pushing the open country a few miles farther away.

I could also see my elementary school in the photo from the 1960s, and next to it a triangular farm field that took its shape from the railroad tracks that cut diagonally across the old grid of country roads. In the spring of my fifth-grade year, as I was about to move on to the middle school across town, my teacher informed the class that the field had been sold to a developer. That summer, my friends and I spent an afternoon playing in a length of sewer pipe that had been buried in the ground but left open at both ends. I was impressed by its size; if I remember correctly, we could ride our bikes through it. By the fall, though, the sewer line was completed and buried, and streets had been laid out and paved.

Then, for several years, nothing happened.

By the time I was twelve, I had taken up a pastime few of my peers shared or understood: birding. One cloudy and chilly morning in early spring, I slung my new binoculars around my neck and struck out for the triangular field by the school. I ignored the empty streets, and walked instead over the dry, brown weeds and ice-crusted snow towards a line of old trees.

On the way, I was startled by a wild and unfamiliar call. Crouching and stalking as best I could, I chased the call across the field. I was rewarded with the glimpse of a wild eye staring back at me through the weeds and the noisy flight of a large bird with a long tail. It was a ring-necked pheasant, a new addition to my life list.

In the summer of that same year, the field was well on its way to becoming a meadow. The dew was heavy on the ground one early morning, and my shoes and pant legs were drenched as I hunted, binoculars at the ready. Again, I was rewarded by the sight of something new.

Electric lines had already been buried in the field, awaiting the arrival of televisions and microwave ovens, so the meadow was dotted with light green posts, about two feet tall, with labels warning of high voltage and the hidden danger of underground wires. Perched on top of one of these posts was a small sparrow of some sort. As I watched, the bird threw back its head and sang. I was expecting a full-throated warble but heard instead a thin, high trill in two parts, like breathing in and breathing out.

I was not the best or most patient of birders, largely because I was too intent on adding to my life list. I restrained myself only long enough to note the bird's markings and to think of a way of describing its strange song ('like breathing in and breathing out') before I pulled out my field guide and tried to pin a name on this new find. There it was: a savannah sparrow. Although I could see the bird was native to North America, the name spoke to me of someplace more exotic, the grassy plains of Africa I had seen on television.

All that summer, on walks and bike rides, I would listen for a thin, two-part trill in the weeds, thinking vaguely of Africa. Then someone mowed the field, and I neither saw nor heard the savannah sparrow again. Not long after that, construction began in earnest, and it seemed only a matter of months before every trace of the meadow was gone. The photo from the late 1990s shows a triangular neighborhood of single-family homes with manicured lawns and trees already approaching maturity.

This was my first direct encounter with environmental change, and I reacted with grief and indignation: grief at the loss of habitat for the native-exotic birds I had discovered, and indignation at the unseen forces of development, those persons unknown who seemed blind and deaf to the qualities of resurgent nature.

Stories of change and loss are common in the suburbs, and my own story now strikes me as a little bit trite. Looking back, I can also see how my reaction was exaggerated or, at least, misdirected. At the time, the situation seemed simple and the appropriate response seemed obvious: the meadow and its inhabitants had been good, and they had been destroyed; this was clearly an occasion for righteous anger. Now I can see the situation was really very complex, and the appropriate response not at all obvious.

For example, one of the values I thought had been destroyed was that of wild nature, the presence of untamed and untrammeled life just a short walk from my home. But the meadow that grew up in the field during that one season was hardly a remnant of the original swampy wilderness of northwest Ohio, even if it was an early step in the succession from cultivated field to second-growth forest. From the structure of the soil, to the hydrology of the surrounding landscape, to its very shape, the triangular field as I encountered it had already been changed and changed again by human activity. The ancestors of the ring-necked pheasant, that prized addition to my life list, had been introduced to North America from Asia by the descendants of Europeans so they could have something interesting to shoot at.

Then there is the fact that I myself was living in a house built on what had recently been a farm field, and that savannah sparrows might have sung from fence posts along the gravel road that once ran where my family had installed our swimming pool. The families who were soon to move into the new neighborhood would probably be just as content with their houses and lawns as we were with ours. The children of those families would ride their bikes, play with or avoid one another, go to the mall on weekends, and watch too much television.

Even if my family was complicit in the process of suburbanization that even now continues to convert fields and forests into subdivisions, at the time I myself played no active role in the process. I was a spectator. I could only watch the triangular field turn into a neighborhood and think someone, somewhere, had made a bad decision.

I am no longer just a spectator. In small ways, at least, I am now myself complicit in environmental change. The decisions I make about where and how to live, how and how much to care for my property, which plants to cultivate and which to kill, what and how much to consume, how to get to work and to the store, which candidates to support for which public offices, and so on, all have some impact on the shape of my environment and the direction in which it changes. While there is still a great deal of environmental change that is beyond my control, I must still observe and judge my own decisions and their consequences, measuring them against my own standards of what is good and what is right.

I tell this story because, in a sense, this book has its start in my memories of that triangular field and in my response to a series of aerial photographs. There is more to the story of how this book came about, of course. For one thing, the timing was important.

When I first saw the photographs, I had already spent more than a decade engaged in the peculiar academic enterprise known as environmental ethics, which can loosely be understood as a way of asking critical questions about what is good and what is right in decisions concerning environmental change. My early work as a philosopher was taken up with offering a critique of the mainstream approach to environmental ethics, with its leaning towards meta-ethical theory and its emphasis on establishing the intrinsic value of natural organisms and natural systems. I aligned myself instead with a number of environmental ethicists who argue for a much more practical, policy-oriented, and frankly human-centered approach to environmental decision making.

By the end of the 1990s, I was prepared to leave behind the critical phase of my project and move on to something more constructive. I thought I should aim to make a direct, practical contribution to some area of environmental policy. In short, I needed a real-world issue, something that really mattered to people, so I could see whether academic ethical inquiry could actually help people make better decisions. I cast about for a while – water supply? energy? agriculture? – but nothing really caught my imagination.

Then, at some point, I remembered the triangular field and my early experience of environmental change. I thought: Why not suburbs?

I was hooked.

Many environmentalists and most environmental ethicists focus on the process of suburbanization – which I now call 'metropolitan growth' – only long enough to point out how awful it is. After all, suburbanization has been one of the most important drivers of environmental change in the United States since at least the 1940s, and mainstream environmental ethicists are predisposed to see most environmental change as change for the worse. What matters, from their perspective, is that expanding development destroys wild and rural landscapes, and it encourages ways of living that are more broadly destructive of 'the environment'.

I had already openly questioned some of the assumptions behind mainstream environmental ethics, including the widespread assumption that wilderness is the standard against which all landscapes are to be measured. I had also questioned the common practice of referring to 'the environment' as though it were a single thing, a non-human other that can be damaged or destroyed as soon as humans touch it.

What I found most compelling about focusing on suburbs, then, was the thought that suburban or metropolitan landscapes are themselves the environments of immediate concern to most Americans, environments that should be taken seriously in their own right. When people make decisions about environmental change, it seemed to me, the degree to which their environment departs from some original wilderness condition is, at most, one consideration among many, and usually not the most important consideration. This struck me as entirely appropriate.

It was at about this point that I first saw the aerial photographs of my old neighborhood and started seriously to rethink my early reaction to the development of the triangular field. Not long after that, the outlines of my approach to the ethics of metropolitan growth came sharply into focus.

To see metropolitan landscapes with clear eyes, and to make decisions about them with clear heads, we need to consider very seriously what may be good about them as well as what may be bad. We need also to be as precise as we can in distinguishing all the different ways in which a landscape and our way of living in it may be good or bad. Then, when we deliberate about what to do in a particular case, we can work towards a rich understanding of what is at stake and a detailed understanding of both the roots of disagreement and the possibility for common ground.

This book is a distillation of what I have learned, so far, about how to identify and distinguish the values and obligations that are in play when we decide how to shape our environment and how to live in it. I offer it in the hope it will help people, on their own and in their communities, to see their own environment more clearly and to make more thoughtful decisions about its future.

Acknowledgments

I owe thanks to many people for helping me along with my exploration of ethics in the built environment, starting with my cousin, Drew Sager, who sent me the aerial photos.

For encouragement and advice in the earliest phases of the project, I am especially grateful to Ed Casey, Bob Mugerauer, Ingrid Stefanovic, Steve Vogel and other colleagues in the International Association for Environmental Philosophy. For more detailed comments and suggestions on various papers and drafts of papers, thanks go to my colleagues Jason Borenstein, Susan Cozzens, Michael Hoffmann, Bryan Norton, and to the late and much-lamented Jon Johnston. I am also grateful to Diana Hicks, Chair of the School of Public Policy at Georgia Tech, for a teaching release during the spring semester of 2005 that allowed this project to advance.

Chapters 4 and 5 have been expanded from research I conducted in 2003 with the support of a Summer Stipend from the National Endowment for the Humanities. I owe Ann Bostrom thanks for pushing me to take what was an abstract conceptual framework for ethics in the built environment and turn it into an empirical research project . . . though I still will not do coding.

An earlier version of Tables 4.1, 5.2 and 5.3 appeared in Robert Kirkman (2004), 'The Ethics of Metropolitan Growth: A Framework', *Philosophy & Geography* 7.2, 201–18. Also, an earlier version of some of the material in section 5.3, including my adaptation of the 'layer-cake' model, appeared in Robert Kirkman (2005), 'Ethics and Scale in the Built Environment', *Environmental Philosophy* 2, 38–52.

Chapter 6 has been informed in part by my collaboration with Doug Noonan on technology, urban form, and the limits of ethics, including research we have conducted under a grant from the National Science Foundation (SES-0646739). The discussion of impure agency in sections 6.1 and 6.2 appears in a different form in Robert Kirkman (2008), 'Failures of Imagination: Stuck and Out of Luck in Metropolitan America', *Ethics, Place and Environment* 11.1, 17–32. The discussion of actor-network theory in section 6.2.c appears in a different form in Robert Kirkman, 'At Home in the Seamless Web: Agency, Obduracy and the Ethics of Metropolitan Growth', *Science Technology & Human Values* 34.2, 234–58.

Introduction

This book is about the decisions we make that shape our built environment, from everyday decisions of home-owners and commuters to grand gestures of national policy. Here is a commuter faced with the choice of driving alone to work, joining a carpool, or using public transit. There is a home-owner trying to decide whether to renovate her current home or move to a new house in the outer suburbs. Meanwhile, a home-owners' association is deciding how strictly to enforce a covenant restricting the size and placement of flower beds, and a zoning board is deciding whether to grant the variances required for an innovative mixed-use development. Elsewhere, a developer has to choose whether to include affordable housing in a new subdivision. Far away, in the capitol, a legislator considers whether to introduce a bill that would impose a heavy tax on gasoline while subsidizing public transit.

As of this writing, such decisions have become more complicated and some of them have become more urgent. The financial crisis that began in 2008 with the collapse of securities backed by sub-prime home mortgages in the United States has expanded, feeding a cycle of home foreclosures and job losses that shows little sign of abating. While energy prices are, for the moment, relatively low, there have been recent signs of instability in the market for the fossil fuels that make the contemporary metropolis possible. All of this is compounded by growing evidence of human-induced climate change, which is likely to make ever more unstable the environmental conditions on which metropolitan life depends.

In response to these new conditions, policy makers have focused on stabilizing the financial system, boosting economic activity, and encouraging the development of clean and renewable energy sources and more efficient technology. The unstated goal seems to be to return as quickly as possible to the way things were before the crisis, to get people to buy houses and cars again, to resume construction of subdivisions and strip malls. It strikes me, however, that the current financial and economic turmoil might also be the occasion for us to take a hard, critical look at the way things have been, particularly the way we have organized our built environment, in light of more basic goals. If the processes that have made the contemporary metropolis what it is seem, for the moment, to have slowed or even halted, then we may have a chance to consider whether to change those processes so they will push in a different direction when they start up again. We may have a chance, in other words, to make thoughtful, deliberate decisions about what we want our built environment to become.

The premise of this book is that all such decisions about the built environment have ethical dimensions that are sometimes hard to see, ethical dimensions that ought to be brought to light, scrutinized, and discussed.

People often bristle at the suggestion that ethics has anything to do with where we choose to live and what we choose to build there. We want what we want, many would protest, and so long as we do not commit any grievous sins or violate any laws no one can tell us not to go after what we want. I may prefer a house in the suburbs over an apartment in the city, or vice versa, and there are no grounds for anyone to criticize my preference. From this perspective, the relevant questions are: How can I maximize satisfaction of my preferences in the marketplace? How can I push my interests in the political arena so the government either helps me to satisfy my preferences or stays out of my way while I do so? Questions of right and wrong do not enter into it.

This objection arises in part from an understanding of ethics quite different from what I have in mind. For many, ethical judgment is bound up with accusation, guilt, and punishment for those who violate moral rules. The most important moral rules seem to be those having to do with death, sex, and truth, and so the most weighty violations are murder, adultery, and lying. Driving alone to work or building a cul-de-sac subdivision of million-dollar homes has nothing at all in common with murdering someone or committing adultery and lying about it, the argument might go. So, to raise ethical questions about the ordinary decisions that shape the built environment is to introduce accusation and guilt where they have no place.

As I understand it, though, ethics is not a fixed set of rules to which we must all conform in order to avoid accusation, guilt and punishment. Rather, it is a form of inquiry, a way of asking critical questions about what is good and what is right as we make decisions. On this understanding, ethics enters into discussions about the built environment as soon as we acknowledge that preferences are not simply given, that we can offer reasons why some preferences may be better than others, and that even our most mundane actions can have good or bad motives, good or bad consequences.

To make a decision is to start on a project, a course of action that leads towards a particular goal. The decision may have been reached carefully or carelessly, revealing something of the character of the decision maker. The goal of the project may or may not be motivated by some understanding of what is good and what is right – a sense of obligation, perhaps, or a vision of the best kind of life for human beings – and that understanding itself may be more or less coherent, more or less defensible. People may disagree as to whether the goal of the project is really worth pursuing, and they may offer reasons for their disagreement. Whatever the worthiness of the goal or the motivation of those who pursue it, carrying out the project itself can set in motion a chain of events that has consequences for others, harming them or helping them in ways that are sometimes surprising. When I say decisions have an ethical dimension, then, I mean we might make better decisions if we were to think carefully and critically about the ends and means of our projects, and about matters of character, motivation, and consequence.

Making decisions through critical ethical inquiry is difficult, to say the very least. People who come together to make a decision may find not only that they judge particular situations and actions differently in reference to different standards, but that the standards themselves are informed by very different views of what it means to be a human being and to live a good human life. This is plainly seen in many divisive social issues, from abortion to immigration, when the two sides often seem as though they were living in different worlds. Debates over metropolitan growth in the United States may be somewhat less heated, but they follow a similar pattern: one person can look at a picture of an urban street and see a vibrant economic and cultural life, while another can look at the same picture and see only filth and the threat of being mugged or swindled; each might think the other is deluded.

Another difficulty for ethical deliberation is that the situations in which we make decisions are usually complex and ambiguous, which can make it difficult to sort out what is good and what is bad in the situation so we can know what to make better and what to leave alone. Consider that our built environment has been shaped by countless human choices, but those choices were guided and motivated by a wide range of values and visions; many of those choices have had unintended consequences. More than this, our built environment is not a pure expression of human values and visions, but is rather the product of a tangled web of natural, social, and technological dynamics. So, as we set out to make our own choices within and about our built environment, each of us is likely to find things we judge to be good and things we judge to be bad all mixed up together. We may even find features of our built environment we judge to be both good and bad at the same time.

The purpose of this book is to provide some practical guidance for sorting through the ethical complexity of the built environment. It does not provide answers – it is not my place to dictate to others the right way to live in the world – but it provides a set of questions that, I hope, can help people make better and more thoughtful decisions. At the core of the book is a framework I intend as a comprehensive set of ethical questions about the built environment: these are things we should pay attention to as we work, alone and together, to figure out which projects to pursue and which to avoid.

I am especially interested in decisions about metropolitan growth in the United States, so the cases and examples to which I refer are largely drawn from American cities and suburbs. This is the context I know best, my native habitat, but that is not the only reason for me to focus close to home.

The landscape of the United States has undergone an extraordinary transformation since the establishment of the first commuter suburbs in the nineteenth century. Compact walking cities and small towns have given way to vast metropolitan regions that have continually extended their reach into the surrounding countryside. The fabric of the resulting metropolis is varied, from high-density inner cities to ultra-low-density outer suburbs, also known as 'exurbs', all tied together by transportation and communications networks. Other cities in other countries have also expanded, but the American pattern of growth is distinctive in its style and in its intensity.

There is much at stake in deciding the future of the built environment in the United States. The degree to which Americans have become dependent on the private automobile, for example, poses a serious challenge to the sustainability of our current ways of building and living. People in other countries have generally been less dependent on the automobile, but are becoming more so. They may learn much from observing the choices Americans make about transportation, and the lessons Americans learn – or fail to learn – from them.

More broadly, I think I have some grounds to hope the framework I present here may prove useful in any context where people are making decisions about their built environment, even if I do take metropolitan growth in the United States as my case study. For that matter, a time may come – assuming it is not already at hand – when Americans themselves will have to consider the ethics of metropolitan retreat or metropolitan reconfiguration rather than metropolitan growth. After Hurricane Katrina devastated New Orleans we may even have glimpsed, if only for a moment, the possibility of an ethics of metropolitan abandonment. The point is that any action or policy that will bring about changes in the built environment can be subjected to critical scrutiny, and such scrutiny can usefully be guided by the same kinds of questions I would have us ask about recent patterns of metropolitan growth in the United States.

In Chapter 1, I set out in more detail my view of ethics as a form of inquiry regarding human projects, and I offer some practical help getting started. In particular, I lay out a set of general questions we should ask about any given project, including questions about ends and means, motives and consequences, and the relations of projects to one another.

I then turn, in Chapter 2, to consider ethical deliberation in its environmental context. A project always unfolds in a particular place, which provides opportunities for and imposes constraints upon choice and action. I pose a set of questions about the relationship between projects and places that may be important for decision making. Along the way, I suggest it can be useful to think of the opportunities and constraints in a particular place as being shaped by a complex interaction of natural, social, and technological dynamics. In Chapter 3, I use this approach to sketch out the dynamics that have given American metropolitan regions their distinctive character.

The pivotal moment of the book comes in Chapter 4, where I set out a comprehensive framework for the ethics of metropolitan growth. I follow up, in Chapter 5, with a demonstration of how the framework might be used in particular cases.

I close, in Chapter 6, by considering the scope and limits of moral responsibility in the built environment. The process of growth is bigger than any one of us, and it is not at all clear that even the best decisions made for the best of reasons will actually do much to change the built environment for the better. Worse, to the extent we already have commitments within our environment, and to the extent our understanding of what is possible has been shaped by our environment, it is not at all clear we are free to make the best decisions for the best of reasons. I argue that, even though we should acknowledge these limits of ethics, we nonetheless have a responsibility to keep looking for better, more just, and more sustainable ways to live in the world.

1. Ethics

Many of the decisions people make about how to structure and how to live within the built environment are ethical decisions, or at least they are decisions that have ethical concerns mixed up in them. All I mean by this is that, to make such decisions well, people need to ask and answer questions about values and obligations: What is good? What ought I to do? What do I owe to myself and to others?

There is widespread disagreement not only about the answers to these questions, but also about what the questions mean and whether it is appropriate to ask them in particular circumstances. My purpose in this chapter is not to present my own resolution to such disagreements, nor even to suggest the one correct perspective from which disagreements may be resolved. Rather, I aim only to encourage open deliberation through which people may resolve disagreements for themselves, and to provide some practical advice for getting started. In particular, I suggest a way of understanding where moral disagreement comes from and the sorts of questions we should ask when trying to work through it.

What I have in mind is an experiential approach to ethics, that is, an approach that starts with ordinary lived experience of the world around us. The world of our experience is packed full of details, and no one is able to pay attention to all of them at once. Our minds have to pick and choose among things and events by using various filters, which cognitive scientists call 'conceptual schemas' or 'mental models'.[1] It is through these filters that we make sense of our experience, picking out what is worth paying attention to from the countless details that may safely be ignored, forging meaningful connections between one detail and another. These meaningful connections lie at the roots of ethical judgment and practice.[2]

Moral disagreement arises because the process of making sense of our experience leaves each of us with a view of the world that is necessarily partial and selective: you pay attention to things I ignore, and vice versa, and we connect things together in different ways that lead us to value them differently. Moral disagreement can be difficult to deal with because I may be utterly convinced that my partial and selective view of the world is complete, perfectly natural, and universally true, and you may have the same conviction about your view even though it is incompatible with mine.

The point of ethics is not just to describe and explain the divergence of partial worldviews, however, and it is certainly not to accept the incompatibility of worldviews with a shrug of the shoulders. Instead, the point is to ask critical questions about each view, to examine its scope and its limits, to test whether it holds together and whether it can be put into practice.

But then, in order to test a worldview, it seems we need some way to step outside it, some way to measure it against a standard that is not itself a part or product of the worldview. Human history and the efforts of philosophical ethicists, however, give us little reason to hope for a single, correct standpoint from which to judge all partial worldviews. Given the limits of human cognition, it seems unavoidable that what we would be stepping into would be just another partial and selective worldview. How, then, is critical ethical inquiry supposed to work?

In practice, each of us always begins ethical inquiry from within our own partial view of the world. From that starting point, we may be able to develop our moral imagination, to work towards an understanding of the world that is richer and more varied, or at least less incomplete, than what we have now.[3] One way to do this is to project ourselves, as much as we can, into other people's points of view, to imagine how the same situation might look and what ethical response it might evoke could we see it through their eyes. In doing this we may discover the limitations of our own understanding, our habitual blindness to particular features of the world that may be worth attending to. There may be many ways to arrive at this kind of insight, but one of the most direct is just to talk to other people.

The experiential approach to ethics implies that each of us should be modest about our own perspectives and judgments. It is not as though one of us sees perfectly while others stumble around in the dark. In a sense, we are all stumbling around. In trying on other people's perspectives, though, we may just discover new ideas and new connections that can help us more thoughtfully and responsibly to make our way in the world. We might even find ways to stumble along in the same direction as other people, helping one another along, even if we have different reasons for going that way.

When all is said and done, there will still be disagreements, likely even entrenched and angry disagreements. Even so, the process of questioning ourselves and one another may lead to a better understanding of where those disagreements come from and how we may be able to work around them in order to pursue common projects.

The notion of a *project* turns out to be especially useful for an experiential approach to ethics. A project is just something a person sets out to do in order to achieve a particular goal. Projects may be big or small, short term or long term, pursued by individuals or by groups. Projects range from the profound to the trivial, from the essential to the optional: the lifelong quest to live a good and decent life is a project, but so is going to the store to buy milk. For that matter, ethical inquiry is itself a project.

Table 1.1 gathers together a set of six questions we might ask about any given project in the course of ethical inquiry. The first three questions are concerned with the value of the project itself, including the means and ends of the project and how the

Table 1.1

Six Questions about Projects

How was the project chosen?
Are the goals of the project worth reaching?
Are the means used to reach the goals of the project appropriate?
Does the project conflict with projects other individuals or groups are pursuing?
Does the project conflict with other projects the same individual or group is pursuing?
Is the project self-defeating?

Table 1.2

Three More Questions about Projects

What is the character of the person pursuing the project?
What is the motivation behind the project?
What consequences follow from the project?

decision was made to pursue the project. The last three questions focus on the relationship of the project to other projects, including its relationship to itself. Projects may mesh together in such a way that pursuing one makes it easier to pursue others, but they can also clash with one another. In such cases, ethical inquiry can slip into something very like a process of conflict resolution.

Discussion around these six questions can be further enriched by weaving in three more questions, gathered in Table 1.2, about how we evaluate the means and ends of a project. Philosophers who work on ethics often distinguish three traditional approaches to evaluation: virtue ethics focuses on the character of the person pursuing the project, deontology or duty ethics focuses on the motivations that lie behind the project, and utilitarianism or, more broadly, consequentialism focuses on the consequences that follow from the project.[4]

In broadest terms, character is a set of consistent and enduring tendencies to act in particular ways; it is what we come to expect of a person based on what we know of the history of what that person has done or said. If someone starts pursuing a project we did not expect of them, we would say she or he is acting 'out of character', which could be good or bad, depending on what we think of that person's character in the first place.

Virtues are those character traits considered to be good or admirable, vices are those considered to be bad or contempt- ible. As with every other part of ethics, there is a long history of disagreement about which traits are which. In Aristotle's virtue ethics, moral virtue is moderation in how a person responds to emotions: courage, for example, is the mean between cowardice and rashness as a response to fear.[5] The virtues Aristotle praises are those that serve the active political and military life of an Athenian citizen, including appropriate degrees of ambition, self- regard, anger, and responsiveness to pleasure. These seem to be firmly at odds with some of the virtues of the early Christian tradi- tion, which are aimed instead at service to God: patience, humil- ity, forebearance, and asceticism. Each tradition seems to take as vices at least some of what the other takes as virtues.

There may still be some virtues on which there is broad agree- ment. Both the Greek and Christian traditions might agree that courage is a virtue, though courage may serve different ends. Integrity is another virtue that is easy to agree on, a kind of com- pleteness and consistency in character, though again this may serve different ends. There are also virtues that have to do with how people go about making decisions, what in the Aristotelian tradition is called 'practical wisdom'.[6] Put simply, this is a matter of being thoughtful and careful in making decisions, and of culti- vating an ability to see what is the appropriate course of action in a given situation.

Turning to the features of a project itself, to ask after the moti- vation for a project is to ask what the person pursuing it has in mind. Is the project intended to serve a higher principle? Is it intended to serve only the interests of the person pursuing it? Are the motives behind the project mixed or confused?

The philosophical touchstone for examining motives is the work of Immanuel Kant, who held that an action can be considered morally good only if it is motivated entirely by duty. As far as Kant is concerned, it is not enough that an action happens to be consistent with duty. If I tell the truth because I am afraid of being caught in a lie, or because I want to be admired for my honesty, or because telling the truth makes me feel good, or because it never occurs to me to do otherwise, then Kant would insist that my action does not really have any moral worth, even if the consequences of the action are the same in every case. My action counts as morally good only if I tell the truth deliberately out of respect for universal moral law, which demands the truth.

This is a hard doctrine, one that is notoriously difficult to live up to in practice. Kant introduces another way of looking at motivation and moral obligation that is perhaps more useful: we ought always to respect other people. For Kant, this means we should recognize that other people are free moral agents, which is to say they are able to formulate their own general rules of conduct and pursue their own projects. Because people are free, Kant argues, we should treat them as ends in themselves, never only as means to our own ends.[7] If I lie to other people, I am in effect coercing them to do what I want by manipulating their understanding of the relationship between us and the situation we are in; I am undermining their freedom and their dignity, violating their basic moral rights, by using them for my own purposes.

After virtue and motivation, the third traditional approach to evaluation considers instead the consequences of a project, the various ways in which the project benefits and harms those affected by it. In deciding whether to pursue a project we need to predict, based on past experience and whatever knowledge of cause and effect we have available, what is likely to happen once the project is under way. To evaluate a project already under way, we need to go out and look at what actually does happen, which may or may not be as we predicted.

If two people each give a large cash gift to the same charity, a consequentialist would say their acts have exactly the same moral worth if the two gifts bring about the same amount of benefit to other people. It may be that one gift is used to give a lot of help to a few people and another is used to give a little help to a lot of people, but that does not matter so long as the total benefit is the same in the two cases. It also does not matter that one person was acting on the principle that everyone ought to help others in need while the other was just out for a quick tax deduction.

There is also a lot of room for debate here, including debate on the question of what is to count as a benefit. For the classical utilitarians Jeremy Bentham and John Stuart Mill, pleasure is the one thing they can identify as good in itself,[8] but it is far from clear that everyone would or should agree on what is pleasurable. More recent versions of utilitarianism take the satisfaction of preferences as good in itself, which acknowledges that people may have different preferences. If monetary values are taken as a way of measuring satisfaction, then the evaluation of projects becomes a matter of cost-benefit analysis.

Each of these three traditional approaches has, at one time or another, been presented as the one true and objective standard for ethical evaluation. It should not come as a surprise that I think of them instead as partial views and that, as a consequence, I do not think it necessary to choose one of them as the only mode of evaluation. In practice, each perspective picks out an important dimension of human moral experience; each can inform and enrich moral imagination. There is some value, then, in having all three at our disposal when we are trying to figure out what to do. Put simply, character, motivation, and consequences all matter to us when we try to figure out whether a project is worth pursuing.

1.1. How was the project chosen?

There may actually be a more basic question lurking here: *Was* the project chosen? Choice implies a deliberate decision to pursue one project rather than another, a decision for which it is possible to give reasons. In that light, then, there do seem to be

projects we pursue without having chosen them. Some of these
are projects that are basic to remaining alive, projects we have
in common with other living things. Breathing is one example.
There are other very basic projects about which we may have
some degree of freedom, but in which our choices may be constrained in various ways. We all have to eat in order to carry out
the basic project of staying alive. We have some latitude in how
we go about eating, but we are still driven by a basic urge and
constrained by what is available, by what we know how to do, by
cultural norms, and so on.

We may also find ourselves pursuing more distinctly human
projects we have never really chosen for ourselves: we just fall into
them as a result of habit, inattention, misdirection, or the prompting of others. Parents choose projects for their children – getting
an education, for example, or following a particular career path,
or developing a taste for a particular style of neighborhood – long
before children are able to decide for themselves. As those children
grow to adulthood, they may hold on to some of their parents'
projects simply because it never occurs to them to do otherwise.

There is also always the possibility of coercion, whether by
force or by fraud. Coercion is itself a project, which aims to get
other people to do things against their will. If force is the means,
then the trick is to threaten a project that is important to them,
including the basic project of staying alive, in order to get them
to carry out a project they would never have chosen on their own.
If fraud is the means, as already noted, the trick is to get them
to make a choice based on a false understanding of the situation they are in. In either case, the victims of coercion have not
freely chosen the projects they are pursuing. Much of the ethical
scrutiny – and much of the blame – shifts to the character and
the motives of the person carrying out the coercion, who is using
other people as mere means.

Setting all of this aside, suppose I choose a project on my own,
without coercion or prompting from other people. I may be more
or less careful in making my choice. I may gather and sort as

much information as I can about the circumstances and possible consequences of the project. I may ask other people for advice to be sure I have not missed anything important or deceived myself in any way. I may be scrupulous in weighing all the ethical implications of the project, as seen from a number of different perspectives. Then again, I may act on impulse, going after the first project that appeals to me, regardless of circumstances or consequences. For that matter, I may just flip a coin.

There is something to be said for any of these options: it is possible to be too deliberate in making a decision just as it is possible to be too impulsive, depending on the situation. There may even be a few situations in which a coin flip is as good a way to decide as any. As a matter of character, at least part of the virtue of making decisions lies in responding appropriately to the situation, gearing the degree and kind of deliberation to the importance and scope of the decision. For any project that is likely to have serious consequences for other people, or in which the rights of other people should be taken into account, we should probably weigh the decision very carefully.

Many of these same considerations apply to decisions about projects that are to be pursued by groups, but with some added wrinkles. In such cases, there are also questions of legitimacy: Who has the right and the authority to decide on behalf of a group? This is an important question for any member of the group who may disagree with a decision but who may nonetheless be bound to go along with it. The question is especially pressing where political authority is concerned and decisions can be backed up by force of arms, if necessary.

In the context of a democratic republic like the United States, how a political decision is made depends very much on the kind of decision it is and the context in which it is to be made. Some decisions are to be made by popular vote or by some other process in which the public participates directly, some decisions are to be made by elected officials in various combinations, and some are left to appointed officials and civil servants.

Decisions made by elected and appointed officials raise many of the same sorts of questions as decisions made by individuals: Was the decision made carefully or carelessly? Was reasonable care taken to protect the rights of others and to ensure they are not unduly harmed? Since people with political authority are in effect making decisions for the entire body politic, however, there are further questions about their character: Do we have reason to trust their judgment? Do they show integrity in conducting the public business? Are they honest in telling the public about what they have done? Have they avoided any possible conflicts of interest?

When decisions call either for a popular vote or for some other kind of public input, there are further questions about degrees of participation and about the inclusion or exclusion of individuals or groups. In principle, popular decisions are more legitimate when a higher proportion of the citizenry participates in the process, and when they make informed and thoughtful decisions. I may cast my vote on the basis of careful research and reflection or on the basis of indifference or habit. Many of my fellow citizens opt out of the process altogether, never bothering to come to the polls; in effect, they have excluded themselves from the process of making a decision they will still have to live with. There is also a long history of cases in which particular individuals or groups have been excluded from participation, whether by law or in spite of the law: they may be kept away by force or by fraud, or they may have other kinds of barriers thrown or simply left in their way that may discourage them from participating.

1.2. Are the goals of the project worth reaching?

Another way of asking this question is: What is the project good for? Every project has a goal or set of goals – to bring about a particular state of affairs that supports some further project, for example. To say a project is good is to say it is good for achieving its particular goal, which leads us to ask whether the goal is itself good. A project is worth doing only if its goal or end is worth reaching.

This is where things can get complicated: the goal of a project may be worth reaching only to the extent it is good for supporting projects aimed at some further goal, which may in its turn be good for supporting still further projects, and so on. Aristotle wrote of a hierarchy of goals or ends: pursuing the art of bridle-making is good to the extent it serves the ends of horsemanship, which is good to the extent it serves the ends of military strategy, which is good to the extent it serves the ends of defending the city-state. But where do all of these ends end?[9]

Aristotle introduces the idea of something that is an end in itself, a highest good about which we can no longer no longer ask, 'What is it good for?' It is simply good in and of itself, without any further qualification. Aristotle's conception of the highest good is often translated as 'happiness', but this can give modern readers the wrong impression. To be happy is in this sense to live an entire life in accordance with virtue, that excellence of the human soul that consists in moderation and practical wisdom in all of our relations with other people in the context of the political community. So, bridle-making and all of the other arts are ultimately aimed at creating and protecting the conditions in which human beings can really thrive as rational animals.[10]

Things get still more complicated at this point, because there is plenty of disagreement about what the highest good really is, perhaps especially among philosophers. For Kant, the highest good is a good will, that is, a will that always chooses duty regardless of other inclinations. Nothing else really matters in saying whether a project is good or bad, least of all whether it will make people happy. For Bentham and Mill, the highest good is pleasure, though Mill is at pains to distinguish between high and low pleasures: high pleasures are those that appeal to the intellect, low pleasures are those that appeal to the flesh.

In each case, the highest good is tied to a particular understanding of what it is to be human and what it is reason is supposed to do. Aristotle, who thinks of us as rational animals, thinks the job of reason is to keep our responses to our emotions in balance. The better we are at maintaining that balance, the better off we are in the long run. Kant seems to think of reason and emotion as much more at odds with one another. Reason works by making general laws – whether laws of physics or moral laws – and we are at our best when reason can impose its law on our conduct in spite of our wayward emotions and merely animal drives.[11] By stark contrast, Bentham and Mill hold that we are most basically pleasure-seekers, and that reason serves to calculate the means of creating the greatest amount of pleasure overall with the least amount of pain. They also hold that reason serves primarily to make sure we are impartial as to who is experiencing the pleasures and pains that result from our actions: another person's pleasures and pains count just as much as mine do in the computation.[12]

What about the rest of us? Most people may not have a single, clear idea of what the highest good is. If you ask them why they did something, they may tell you what they think it was good for. If you ask them what that further goal is good for, they may give a further answer. When pushed still further, many Americans would probably find refuge from your nosiness in something like 'because it makes me happy'. If you are especially rude, or if you are a philosopher, you might ask them why happiness is good. They may answer something like 'because it makes me feel good', which is good because it makes them happy, which is good because it makes them feel good, and on and on. Still, in practice, their projects may be aimed at any of a number of goods other than their own immediate satisfaction, all of them very high if not actually highest: a healthy family life, a strong community, freedom from the interference of a strong community, tranquility, excitement, usefulness to others, a more just society, a secure retirement, victory over the enemy, a more peaceful world, lots of time to play, and many others besides.

What all of this means, in practical terms, is that thinking and talking about the value of any particular project can very easily draw us into a discussion of the most essential questions about human life in the world: What does it mean to be human? What is the best kind of life for a human being? Each of us then has the task of sorting through all of our various goals, seeing how they clash and how they may be reconciled, and deciding which are most important. The most effective way of carrying out this task is in conversation with others, considering their choices and the reasons they offer for them, and allowing our own choices and reasons to be open to the scrutiny of others. This part of ethical inquiry helps us to establish the standard against which the worth of any particular project is to be measured.

In the end, of course, we may all still disagree with one another about which goals are worth reaching and which are not. When a group of people who disagree with one another have to make a decision together about a common project, either they have to find some way of reconciling or at least accommodating their various visions of the good, or they have to devise a way of choosing one vision over all of the others, or they have to agree to go their separate ways. Reconciling visions of the good is the most difficult of these options, especially in a large and diverse republic like the United States: it requires a willingness to see our own highest goals in a new and sometimes harsh light, a willingness to learn from other people and change our minds. It is somewhat easier to accommodate visions without trying to reconcile them. This is the art of compromise, which often has the effect of not really serving anyone's idea of the good. Easier still is simply to let the majority rule in a particular case, though this may have consequences for the coherence of the republic if people in the minority position are particularly outraged by the decision.

1.3. Are the means used to reach the goals of the project appropriate?

The basic question about the ends or goals of the project is: 'Why?' The basic question about the means used to reach those ends is: 'How?' What do we have to do, how do we have to arrange things, for a project to bring about its intended result?

There is usually more than one way of going about pursuing a given project, and some ways are usually better than others. Here again, though, things can get complicated, since there are at least two senses in which one set of means can be said to be better than another. It may be that some means are more effective than others, or it may be that some means are more consistent with other values and obligations, or it may mean both of these together.

To be effective in pursuing a project is actually to be able to arrange things and do things that lead directly to the goal of the project. Not every set of means is equally effective in this sense. There may be a greater or lesser chance of failure. Some means are also more efficient than others, getting the job done with a lower expenditure of time, energy, and resources. In economic terms, efficiency can be expressed in terms of cost-effectiveness, how much bang we get for our buck.

Effectiveness does not really seem to be an ethical matter in itself, unless it can be considered a sort of practical virtue of skill or prudence. Effectiveness could figure in our ethical take on a given project, though, if it has some bearing on other values. In a particular case, effectiveness might serve to prevent harm to other people that would have resulted from failure or waste. In such a case we might say it is good, if only indirectly, to be effective.

It is important to understand, however, that not all effective means are good, which opens up the second and more directly ethical way of evaluating means. In a particular case, the most effective and efficient way of getting to the goal may violate the rights of other people, treating them as mere means to the project's ends, or it may impose undue harms or risks on other people. The old saying that the ends do not justify the means applies here: the nobility of a goal does not make it all right to do anything at all that is needed to reach it. In such a situation, less effective means might actually be better in that they are more consistent with other values and obligations, perhaps based on a standard of reasonable care.

It is not too difficult to imagine a situation in which there is no way to avoid harming someone or violating someone's rights on the way to achieving an important goal. It may be that the harms from one set of means fall on one group while the harms or risks from another set of means fall on another group. We would then be faced with a painful choice: we either have to reconsider the goal and perhaps ultimately stop pursuing the project, or we have to decide how to distribute the harms and risks we cannot avoid. In the best case, perhaps, one individual or group may volunteer to take the hit: a risk that is accepted freely is better than a risk imposed willy-nilly. Barring that, we may find that there really is no best option, only the lesser of evils.

1.4. Does the project conflict with projects other individuals or groups are pursuing?

The fact that a project can impose risks or harms on other people opens up a more general consideration of how projects interact with one another. To pursue a project is to bring about changes in the world for a particular purpose. Those changes set up new conditions that may make it easier or harder to pursue other projects. One person's project of waterskiing on a remote lake is clearly at odds with another person's project of passing an afternoon in quiet contemplation by the shore of the same lake. In the worst cases of ethical and political conflict, one project simply makes it impossible for others to pursue some important project, either taking away some essential means or pushing the goal further out of reach.

At this point, ethical inquiry shifts its focus from the evaluation of individual projects to the sometimes much thornier task of resolving conflicts between people over their various projects.

These conflicts can go deep, as already noted: the people involved may be pursuing very different goals based on a very different understanding of how the world works, how human life fits into the world, and what is really important.

This is also a point at which ethical inquiry can turn back on itself, since resolving conflicts is itself a project open to evaluation: it may or may not be worth doing in a particular case, and it may be done well or poorly. For that matter, there may even be a conflict about whether and how to resolve a conflict. In general, though, good conflict resolution may be taken as a special case of good decision making: we should be thoughtful, we should be creative, and, when we have to make decisions together, we should attend to matters of political legitimacy.

1.5. Does the project conflict with other projects the same individual or group is pursuing?

On any given day, we all pursue a number of different projects, as individuals and in groups, each of which demands some share of the resources available to us, including our time, attention, and effort. This is not a problem if the projects all pull in more or less the same direction, towards a common goal, or if the projects at least do not conflict outright. However, we may find ourselves, as individuals and as groups, engaged in projects that pull in different directions, creating sometimes painful dilemmas: Work overtime or go to a child's piano recital? Design a system to be safe or design it to be inexpensive? Defend national security or protect individual liberties?

Concerning the various projects of individuals, the virtue of integrity is relevant here. The idea of integrity is that a person can and should develop a wholeness of character or a unity of motivation, getting all the other projects of life lined up and pulling towards some overarching goal. This can serve to minimize conflict by weeding out projects that do not fit with the overall plan, and by providing a single point of reference for deciding how much time and effort to give to each of the projects that remain. We generally think of integrity as a good trait for people to have, perhaps especially other people. At the very least, people with integrity can be counted on to be consistent.

What may be generally admired in individuals is much more controversial in the political domain. It is not nearly so clear that all of the various projects pursued by the citizens of a demo-cratic republic should be lined up towards a single, substantive overarching goal, or even that they can be lined up in that way. If we did aim to align all our projects, we would have to regard the body politic as a kind of super-human, with a soul of its own capable of achieving integrity.[13] For good or ill, that kind of unity of purpose is seldom to be found among human beings, even under conditions of tyranny: someone will always disagree and start pulling in another direction. The United States, with its tradi-tion of civil liberty, free enterprise, and free expression, and with its long history of immigration, expansion, and social ferment, has turned out to be wildly diverse and perhaps deeply divided in the ends and means of our many projects.

To be able to live together under a common political order, it seems we do have to agree on at least a few things. At the very least we have to commit to working together by some set of political and legal procedures for resolving, rectifying, or even just containing our various conflicts.[14] How far such an agree-ment needs to go for the political order to remain viable is open to debate. For some, we need to move back towards the remem-bered or imagined cultural unity of the past, while others hold that we should let a thousand flowers bloom. For some, the sole function of government is just to keep us from actually harming one another while we each go about our separate business, while for others the proper function of government includes establish-ing or protecting certain public goods, sometimes at the expense of some private goods. Even among those who agree that the public should act together to protect public goods there is bound to be disagreement over which goods are worth protecting and at what cost.

1.6. Is the project self-defeating?

A further possibility is that a project might conflict with itself, throwing obstacles in its own path. The problem may be that the particular means chosen to reach the goals of the project are limited or fragile, such that to use them is to use them up: once they are gone, the project is over whether the goal has been reached or not. It might also be that the means have particularly bad side-effects that push attainment of the goal further way. Then again, it may be that the goal itself is simply unattainable by any of the available means, so those who pursue the project are doomed always to find themselves falling short or moving in the wrong direction.

Sustainability is a special case of the relationship of a project to itself, usually with a focus on really big projects like the economic development of whole nations or even the vast project of civilization itself. A civilization or an economy is unsustainable to the extent it undermines the conditions of its own continuation, usually understood in ecological terms: it depends on non-renewable resources, for example, or it disrupts the ecological systems that provide it with essential services such as clean water, fertile soil, and a stable climate. The big questions in such cases are whether and how we can move from an economy and a civilization that is unsustainable to one that is sustainable – or at least more sustainable – without losing too much of what we value in the way things are now.

2.   Ethics and Environment

In everyday conversation, people tend to talk about *the* environment, a great big thing about which we have all sorts of opinions. A person may care about the environment or not. Some people may seem only to use or even abuse the environment, while others try to protect it from use and abuse, and a few wait – anxiously or eagerly – for the environment to take its revenge. Our relationship to the environment raises issues or problems over which we wrangle in private conversation, in the political forum, and even in the marketplace. Whatever people think about the environment, in this sense, it is still an *it*, a real thing, or at least a real system of things, that endures over time and has its own distinctive characteristics that are open to scientific investigation. It is stable or it is changeable, depending on whom you ask; it is fragile and endangered, or it is robust and resilient.

One common variant of this way of speaking of the environment implies it is whatever and wherever we are not. People sometimes distinguish the environment from the economy, for example, the same way we sometimes distinguish nature from culture: the relationship between them may be complex and problematic, but they remain two entirely different things. Often, the split runs between the wild and the domestic, leading people to speak of the environment as that which is untouched by human beings. When humans intervene with our various tools to change the environment, the result is somehow no longer the real environment but something else instead. So, people often talk loosely of the ways in which human activities damage the environment, degrade it, or even destroy it.

This way of talking has the peculiar implication that most people do not actually live in the environment, at least not in the kind of environment that really matters. One version of this holds that the few remaining scraps of the true environment are to be found in wild places that few people even see, except as pictures in calendars or on computer desktops. Another version holds that the domesticated human realm is nested within the environment and dependent upon it, but that the environment is still a separate kind of reality. In the actual places we inhabit, what used to be the environment is mangled by bulldozers, buried beneath the streets, or shoehorned into private backyards and fragments of public parkland.

Some of the first efforts to bring ethical inquiry into decisions people make about the environment have often played on this distinction between the wild and the domestic.[1] Academic environmental ethicists have often framed their own work as a matter of discovering or establishing the moral obligations human beings have towards the environment: What do we owe to it? In the spirit of Thoreau's declaration that 'all things good are wild and free', wilderness remains the moral touchstone for many environmental ethicists.[2] For them, pristine environments and wild creatures are more interesting and important than domestic environments and domesticated creatures. The idea that the environment or its various components might have intrinsic value is taken to imply that any mere use we make of them constitutes a degradation or even a desecration. To the extent natural entities and systems are good, we should leave them alone as much as possible.

There is another, perhaps broader, thread in academic environmental ethics that aims towards a reintegration of human society and systems into the natural environment. The model for this is the work of Aldo Leopold, the forester and essayist who proposed a land ethic in the late 1940s. Drawing upon organism and community metaphors in ecology, Leopold suggested that humans should come to see themselves as 'plain members and citizens' of biotic communities, giving up the role of conqueror.[3] The point of this is to see that our domestic realm is enfolded within the environment and intertwined with it, and to see that we have been behaving very badly. In our folly, we have been rearranging components of the environment to suit our own needs, often harming the various organisms who are our fellow citizens even as we harm the stability and integrity of the whole community. Here again, the characteristics of the pristine environment – its stability and integrity – are the moral touchstones for becoming better citizens and creating a domestic realm in harmony with its wild surroundings.

There are some notable problems with thinking of the environment in these terms. For one, it is not always clear how big the environment is supposed to be. In some circumstances it seems fitting to refer to a particular watershed or a particular bioregion as the environment, while in other circumstances the environment may be expanded to include the whole of the biosphere or even, at its furthest extent, the solar system that feeds energy into the biosphere and throws an occasional meteor our way. At the very least, this pushes towards a recognition that there are any number of environments, nested together like the layers of an onion.

For another, whatever the scale, it seems increasingly unlikely the environment has a fixed essence that tends towards one particular state of balance or harmony we might be obligated to preserve or adhere to. From the point of view of ecologists, for example, it turns out that ecological systems are not really all that much like machines, or organisms, or even cybernetic systems, all of which have an identifiable state of proper functioning: good repair, health, and equilibrium, respectively. Ecologists in the past used all of those metaphors to try to pin down the true nature of the larger wholes that emerge from the interactions of living things among themselves and with their physical surroundings, but none of them seems to have stuck as a unifying theory for ecology.[4]

Even setting aside the problem of knowing what the environment is, thinking of the environment as one big thing also presents a problem for the project of investigating the ethics of metropolitan growth. I think of this project as an extension of environmental ethics into the built environment, sorting out the various values and obligations that are at stake when we make decisions within and about the place where we actually live. If we think of humans and our works as separate from and in opposition to the environment, though, then there can be only one outcome of applying environmental ethics to American metropolitan areas: general disapproval.[5] We may disapprove as a matter of absolute principle because a city is not a wilderness, or we may disapprove as a matter of degree because cities and suburbs do not respect or mimic natural harmony the way villages and farms do. There are not many resources here for the sort of fine-grained ethical inquiry I have in mind.

There is another sense of the term 'environment', though, that draws from the root meaning of the term: the environs, that which surrounds a particular thing or group of things. In ecological terms, environment is relative to an organism, comprising other organisms as well as underlying physical and chemical dynamics that support or thwart its projects. Using the term in this sense, we should speak not of *the* environment, but *our* environment – whoever *we* happen to be. I may be concerned most directly with my environment, my family's environment, my community's environment, and so on, or for ethical reasons I may shift my concern to your environment, your family's environment, and so forth. We can even consider, for various reasons, the savannah sparrow's environment as well as those of the fruit fly, the oak tree, the bacillus, and any other living things and perhaps even some larger systems – even some that are not generally thought of as living systems. Meteorologists, for example, will sometimes speak of the environment of a hurricane as either favorable or unfavorable to its continuing development.

Switching from the absolute to the relative sense of 'environment' has a number of advantages, not least of which is that it jibes with our experience of what it is like to live in our environment. In our daily lives, we do not experience our environment as one big thing, or even as a collection of things. Rather, we encounter a complex set of particular things, dynamic patterns, and relationships that present opportunities and impose constraints.[6] Our awareness and understanding of those patterns and relationships, the meaning they hold for us, and the scale at which we pay attention to them are all tied to the projects we happen to be pursuing at the time.[7] If I am trying to swat a mosquito that has made its way into my house, the scale of my environment relative to that particular project shrinks down to the room I am in and the various things around me that can help me or hinder me: a section of newspaper lying on the table becomes a possible weapon while the doorway to the next room becomes a route through which my quarry can escape and the dark furniture becomes a backdrop that makes it hard for me to track its flight. If I am trying to tend a garden, or get to work during rush hour, or protest the planned destruction of a stand of trees, or run a multinational corporation, then the scale, composition, and meaning of my environment all shift accordingly.

Notice that the composition of our various environments is not restricted to natural dynamics of the kind that are studied by the natural sciences. For any one of us at any time, our environment typically includes other human beings pursuing their own projects, and it includes the results of various projects that human beings pursued in the past. So, the underlying dynamics of any given human environment include social and technological dynamics as well as natural dynamics. This means an urban or suburban neighborhood may properly be referred to as a person's environment in precisely the same sense a pristine old-growth forest can be referred to as a spotted owl's environment.

Taking the term 'environment' in its relative sense and acknowledging that cities and suburbs are environments in the fullest sense of the term is likely to raise concerns on the part of many environmentalists and environmental ethicists. From their point of view, the advantage of taking 'environment' in the absolute sense is that it promises an objective standard against which human actions can be measured, a standard that can be used to resolve all public debates about how to live on the land and what to leave alone. If we can show, they might say, that the value we place on a particular patch of woodland is rooted in an underlying principle about protecting the environment, which is rooted in turn in objective knowledge of what the environment really is and what it demands of us, then we can offer a compelling argument as to why that patch of woodland over there should not be cut down to build another big-box 'giga-center'. This is the kind of argument that is supposed to end all debate: if people continue to disagree, they are just being irrational. If we were to accept that 'environment' is a relative term that is tied to individual projects, the objection would conclude, then we have no way of ending debate, no way of convincing people once and for all that environmentalist values and policy proposals should have priority.

For my part, I freely acknowledge this consequence of shifting to the relative sense of environment. But then, I also think the search for the debate-ending argument from nature is not really a very useful enterprise, and is not likely to be successful in any case.[8] Instead, I would work towards an understanding of environmental ethics that is more in line with the idea, introduced in the last chapter, that ethics is a form of inquiry rather than a set of rules. Ethical inquiry is a matter of evaluating and deliberating about human projects through an open process of critical inquiry involving many different frameworks. Environmental ethics is essentially the same, but focused on a narrower set of projects that are tied directly to shaping and reshaping our environments, considered individually and in combination. Of particular interest for environmental ethics are changes to our *common* environment.

Our common environment is the shared field of opportunities and constraints in which our many projects interact with one another, with the projects of other organisms, and with underlying physical dynamics. Someone's project of building a suburban neighborhood on a patch of former farmland changes what is possible for other people in that particular place. A lot of people will be able to live the kinds of lives they value there, but the land will no longer suit people with other projects, a farmer who would use the land to grow crops, for example, or a birdwatcher who would let it go wild to support a more diverse population of bird life.

A situation like this raises an important ethical question: Which projects ought to be given priority? The purpose of environmental ethics, as I understand it, is to *ask* questions like this, critically and persistently, without necessarily presupposing that there will be a unique and universally correct answer. This is not to say that anything goes, however, or that decisions in public or in private will always be perfectly arbitrary. We may not be able to say that a particular project should always have priority as a matter of absolute and universal right but, following guidelines like those set out in the last chapter, we can think and discuss our way to the conclusion that some projects are better than others. The decision to pursue a project may be more or less carefully considered, more or less informed by the diversity of values and perspectives that are at stake, more or less wise; the process of deliberation that leads to the decision may be more or less perceptive, inclusive, critical, rigorous, or honest.

Notice, though, that there is some ambiguity in what is to count as a question for environmental ethics. In the case of building a suburban subdivision, changing the opportunities and constraints of our common environment is a deliberate goal of the project. The same is true of many other projects, from planning a new town to restoring a patch of prairie, from revising zoning regulations to protecting a designated wilderness area. Questions and debates about these kinds of projects are central to what we generally think of as environmental issues.

There are many other cases, though, in which changes to our common environment are the unintended consequences of projects that are aimed at some other goal entirely. Pollution is perhaps the most pervasive example of this. If my project is to get to the store using the means made available to me by my current environment, I may not be thinking at all of the way in which driving to the store may contribute to conditions that interfere with some other people's project of breathing (i.e., ground-level ozone pollution), or to conditions that may complicate everyone's projects, to one degree or another, in the future (i.e., global climate change). Some such cases are also central to what we think of as environmental issues.

In this second set of cases, though, environmental issues overlap or intertwine with other kinds of ethical and social issues. Pushing this to an extreme, even projects that are proposed in response to issues in ordinary human ethics could have the effect of changing the opportunities and constraints offered by our common environment. Consider the controversy over abortion, for example. Abortion involves decisions about human reproduction, which is tied to human population growth, which is tied in turn to the consumption of natural resources, which is tied to sustainability. This may not be saying very much, since the effects are probably very slight and likely only to become more slight with each step. In any case, the question of whether abortion should be legal would not be decided on this basis, but instead by answering questions about the relationships among people, including the question of who counts as a person for the purposes of decision making. So, abortion is not in itself an environmental issue, even if there is an environmental angle on the issue that might serve to complicate – if only slightly – public deliberation about the rights and responsibilities involved in human reproduction.

The 'environmental angle' comes down to a recognition that people always pursue projects in particular places, and that sometimes the relationship between the project and the place matters very much in deciding which projects to pursue and how to pursue them. Place may be more or less important in deciding about a given project, ranging from those that have environmental change or preservation as their explicit goal to those in which place is only a minor and peripheral consideration. Somewhere on this continuum is a blurry line between issues we tend to think of primarily as environmental issues and those that are primarily in some other domain of ethics. I would put the project of driving my car to the store on one side of the line, among environmental issues, and projects related to abortion, affirmative action, and the like on the other.

I use the term, 'place', here as a kind of shorthand for the environment of a person or group of people pursuing a particular project. More precisely, a place is some portion of a person's overall environment that is most immediately relevant to the project at hand. I intend the term to bring together two different ways in which features of a person's environment might be relevant: those that are relevant because they are seen as important by the person pursuing a project, and those that are relevant because they may be changed by the project in a way that affects others and their projects. In other words, 'place' is an ambiguous term, riding the line between *my* environment (as I perceive it) and *our* environment (as my project changes it).

There is always the possibility that my perception and understanding of my place are radically out of step with what actually happens to others and to their projects as a consequence of what I do. I do not see the exhaust fumes coming out of the tailpipe of my car, mingling with the exhaust coming out of other tailpipes and reacting with sunlight to produce ozone. Nor do I see the many children whose asthma is aggravated by the high ozone levels in the region. If I did not become aware of those connections by some other means – scientific research and public information campaigns among them – I could not take them into account when I decide whether to drive to the store. All I would know is that there is no milk in the fridge, there is a car in the

Table 2.1

Three Questions about Place

What is the place in which the project will unfold?
How might the project change this place and its broader context?
How much can we know about how the project will unfold in this place?

---

driveway, and the price of gas is not yet so high I really have to think twice about hopping in the car and going.

I would suggest that thinking carefully about place should be a significant part of ethical deliberation in many cases (see Table 2.1). At the very least, asking critical questions about the context in which a project will play itself out can help to prevent unpleasant surprises, whether in unintended consequences for other people or in the failure of the project itself. More than this, it would not be going too far to say that each of us has a basic ethical responsibility to be as well informed as we can about matters of place, to narrow the gap between our perceived environments and the common environment we share with others. Part of this responsibility is a simple matter of reasonable foresight and reasonable care concerning the consequences of our actions. Another part of it is an ability and a willingness to consider our actions from the point of view of other people who are pursuing other projects for reasons of their own.

2.1. What is the place in which the project will unfold?

The description of a place will always be more than just a catalogue of the people and things that happen to be around, since the meaning and relevance of those things and people can change relative to the project. Instead, it is useful to think of the place as a field of opportunities and constraints that bear directly on the prospects of completing the project. To give a complete answer to this question, then, is to give an account of what would make the project possible and what might block or deflect it. Not only will such an account shed a particular kind of light on people and things, but also on the underlying natural, social, and technological dynamics that connect them together.

The most basic experiences we have of opportunities and constraints in a particular place are rooted in the movement of our bodies.[9] To take a trivial example, I know without thinking about it that I can walk through an open door but not through one that is closed: one is an opportunity, the other a constraint. I also know I can lean on a closed door but not on the space in the middle of an open doorway. Through long experience, and through the systematic investigations of the natural sciences, we can come to recognize other, much more subtle regularities in our experience and even to make predictions about when particular ways may be open to us and when they may be closed. We can also come to understand with some precision the capacities and the limitations of our own bodies.

We know, about as well as we can know anything, that we are bound by gravity, slowed down by friction, compelled to breathe, to drink, and to eat, and caught up in any number of other physical and chemical processes. We also know there is nothing personal in this: human beings have not been singled out for a particular kind of treatment by an arbitrary universe. These same dynamics are at work everywhere, all the time. We are so familiar with them that we seldom think of them unless they happen to get in the way of a particular project: lifting a very large object, for example, or pushing it across the floor. Notice that, in these cases, natural processes such as gravity and friction work as both opportunities and constraints: they keep my feet on the floor and give me something to push against, but they keep the large object in place as well.

There are also natural processes that are less familiar because they come to our attention only once in a while, and we may not be able to see them for what they are without a lot of help from the natural sciences. Consider how Aldo Leopold reinterpreted a turning point in American history in ecological terms. When European settlers moved into the cane-lands of Kentucky, the land responded to their treatment – 'the cow, plow, fire and axe of the pioneer', as Leopold puts it – by producing bluegrass.[10] If the land in that particular place had instead produced plants with no economic value, Leopold suggests, the course of American history might have been very different. Leopold understands land in ecological terms, as a community of living things bound together by flows of energy and matter. The land community in each place is distinctive, the product of a particular intersection of evolutionary, ecological, climatic and geological processes at work in that place.

Relationships among people also give shape to the places where we pursue projects. We can help one another or get in one another's way, both as individuals and through larger social processes. Economic and political systems offer opportunities for action but also impose constraints, channeling our efforts along particular pathways. Take, for example, the very local project of getting to work. The place relative to that project includes roads, curbs, buildings, and fences that are the visible and tangible results of abstract social conventions like private property, rights-of-way, and the institutions that collect tax revenue and fund road construction and maintenance. Lots of people are likely to use these roads at the same time for the same social and economic reasons, leading to traffic congestion that can make it difficult for anyone to get anywhere very quickly.

From the point of view of an individual, the pattern of the roads and the regular incidence of traffic congestion are imposed from without, but some social constraints on action work from within. One of the central tenets of many ethical frameworks is that other people are not to be regarded as just another set of opportunities and constraints relative to our own projects. Instead, there are constraints we ought to place on ourselves in our relationships with others. This can be thought of in different ways: respect for individual persons as ends-in-themselves, for example, or empathy for our fellow humans, or the requirements of membership in the moral community. However conceived, though, such internal restrictions also become part of the place in which a project is to unfold. Some paths are closed to us, not because we cannot go down them but because we ought not to do so.

Technological dynamics shape places as well. In carrying out our projects, we interact with an array of technical artifacts that provide opportunities and constraints of their own. The automobile enables quick and convenient travel from any point in the road network to any other, for example, but it also constrains us to occasionally finding a place to fuel the car and always finding a place to park when we get to our destination. I will say more about technological dynamics in the next chapter.

Another important part of describing a place is specifying the scale, in both space and time, of the dynamics that are most relevant to the project. It would be odd to talk about swatting a mosquito on Earth sometime in the next century, or mitigating the effects of climate change in my living room in the next five minutes. The context for a project may be a room, a household, a neighborhood, a city, a region, a watershed, a nation, a continent, the planet, or any gradation in between. The project itself may span seconds, hours, weeks, months, or years. Most of us, most of the time, are involved in projects at smaller scales, what we casually refer to as the here and now.

We may need to attend to more than one scale at once. The place defined by the scale most relevant to a project is enfolded within and shaped by its own broader context, consisting of dynamics that work at larger scales. It can be helpful to think of a project as resting at the center of a set of concentric rings, with the first ring as the place most immediately relevant to the project and the outer rings representing the broader context with its layers of processes that span longer and longer scales of space and time.[11]

In general, larger-scale processes tend to impose constraints on smaller-scale processes, and changes in smaller-scale processes can have effects that spill over into larger scales.[12] So, celestial processes that operate on the scale of millions of years and geological processes that operate on the scale of millennia impose constraints on climate processes that operate at the scale of decades and centuries, which in turn impose constraints on weather processes that operate at the scale of months and years, which impose constraints on any number of local human projects. Going back the other way, burning fossil fuels to meet the immediate needs of an economy that operates on the scale of days, months, and quarters very likely has spillover effects on climate processes, which are very likely to impose new constraints on local weather and on human projects from year to year over the next few centuries.

2.2. How might the project change this place and its broader context?

Often enough, whether we mean them to or not, our projects end up bringing about changes in the places where they are carried out. To make good decisions about which projects to pursue and how to pursue them, it is reasonable that we should think through what those changes are likely to be, what effects they will have on other projects pursued by other people, and how they may spill over into the broader context.

Many of the most basic human projects are aimed at rearranging or redirecting natural processes for particular human purposes. In the course of a few centuries, a particular patch of land may be transformed from forest to farm to meadow to park to subdivision, with each step in the process intended to open up opportunities for a specific range of projects and to impose constraints on a specific range of other projects.

In ecological terms, this kind of transformation involves breaking up existing relationships among living things and establishing new ones that often involve different kinds of living things.

Following Aldo Leopold, we can think of these relationships in terms of the many particular food chains out of which a land community is constructed.[13] A food chain is nothing more than a record of what eats what, which allows us to trace the flow of energy and matter through ecological systems. To turn a forest into a farm is to introduce new food chains involving exotic species like wheat or soy, pushing aside or destroying old food chains. To turn a farm into a subdivision is to introduce still other, usually much shorter, food chains, pushing aside or destroying still more old food chains.

Meanwhile, the many food chains in which humans participate are spread over wider and wider areas: the food I eat for breakfast on a given morning may include bananas from Mexico, pineapple from Hawaii, oranges from Florida or Texas, wheat from the high plains, cow-milk yogurt from the northeast, and coffee from South America. In this way, the fertility of far-flung places is gathered together in my kitchen and consumed in my dining room. Some of the excess ends up feeding bacteria at a sewage treatment plant several miles from here before making its way into the river and, from there, to the ocean. The banana peels end up in the compost heap in my backyard that will someday contribute to the fertility of the land I live on – though as of now that land produces only plants that are meant to be looked at rather than eaten.

I do not mean to suggest that altering ecosystems to suit human purposes is always a bad thing. I merely propose that we see these alterations for what they are and consider their consequences for ourselves and for others. The success of human projects depends in large measure on the support of ecological systems, if nothing else to provide us with food to eat, water to drink, and air to breathe. How and how much we alter those systems will determine whether and for how long they will provide support for which kinds of projects. In Leopold's terms, there is the real possibility that if the changes we make are too rapid or too widespread, the flow of energy through the land community may be disrupted in a way that reduces the capacity of the land to support diverse living things and diverse human projects.

Spillover effects are especially important in tracing out the consequences of environmental change. Suppose my goal is to have bananas for breakfast because they are convenient and I like the way they taste. In order to get them, however, I have to participate in and contribute to the creation of a system of production and distribution that has national and even global consequences, even if I do not think of myself as doing anything but making breakfast. The banana production system – if I can get away with calling it that – rearranges ecosystems in far-away places I may never see, and shapes the lives and prospects of people I am unlikely ever to meet.

Spillover effects also complicate questions of whether environmental change is intentional. Suppose I introduced an exotic plant to my yard with the explicit intention of altering my immediate environment: the exotic may provide something new to look at, or something new for me to eat. But then suppose the plant's offspring escape the bounds of my garden and the bounds of my intentions, spreading quickly across the region and displacing or killing native plants. I may have intended to change my environment, but not in that way or on that scale. So it was, more or less, with kudzu in the American South, and there are similar stories to tell about many invasive species. Starlings were introduced to North America in the late nineteenth century, legend has it, by a group that wanted only to establish a breeding population in the United States of every bird mentioned in the works of William Shakespeare. The population of starlings exploded across the continent and became a serious agricultural pest and a threat to native songbirds.[14]

As it is with ecological changes to my surroundings, so it is with social and technological changes. Suppose I own a house and the parcel of land on which it sits. I can only do this in the context of a set of political and economic institutions that protect my right to own private property and provide me with the economic means of doing so. My ownership of this house shapes other people's relationships to me: unless they are part of my immediate family, they are not allowed on my property without my explicit permission and, all else being equal, they do not have the power to tell me what to do with my property. I may even put up a tall privacy fence around my property, a technical device that both signals my ownership and enforces the exclusion of others from entering my property or even seeing what I am doing here.

If someone, somewhere, were successful in pushing for a change in how the right to own property is to be interpreted in my jurisdiction, it could significantly alter my relationship with my neighbors and with the broader human community. Suppose the change made the rights of private ownership more subordinate to the public good and created an official mechanism for hearing and acting upon complaints from neighbors. While I may still retain the right, all else being equal, to do what I want with my land, there are suddenly many more instances in which all else is not equal. My neighbors, who had been increasingly annoyed that my fence was ruining what they see as the park-like character of the neighborhood, might finally be able to petition the local government, which might then compel me to take down the fence or face a hefty fine. Of course, all of this could turn the other way if someone, somewhere, were successful in pushing for a more absolute interpretation of property rights.

Social, political, and technological opportunities and constraints may not be distributed equally among people in a particular place or in the broader human community. To be the owner of a piece of land is to have a particular kind of power in relation to other people, backed up by the power of political institutions. If a political and economic system is set up so certain people or groups of people are excluded from owning land or severely restricted as to where they are able to buy land, then their access to that particular kind of power is limited – and so may be their access to other kinds of power besides, at least compared to others living within that same system. Projects that alter local human relationships or spill over into broader political and economic systems can alter this distribution of power, either freeing up those who have been most constrained or constraining them still further.

As with ecological changes, projects can have social and technological consequences beyond anything that was intended. From the point of view of someone buying a car in the 1920s, the goal may be only to have a new way to get around and meet basic needs, or maybe only to feel the excitement of owning something new. Among other things, this purchase added to the growing demand for more and better roads. This demand combined with other economic, political and cultural forces, technological innovation, and a few historical accidents to produce a nation-wide network of highways, roads, and streets that have in turn given American metropolitan areas their distinctive shape. This network has granted unprecedented mobility to those who own private cars, and it has enabled new kinds of social and economic arrangements and spurred further technological innovation. Its construction also tore apart older social and economic relationships within cities and towns, between neighborhoods, and even between neighbors – though more affluent neighborhoods could sometimes avoid the worst of these consequences, at least in the short term.

2.3. How much can we know about how the project will unfold in this place?

Disagreements in matters of ethics and policy sometimes hinge on disagreements about what the consequences will be of a particular course of action. If I hide an uncomfortable truth from a friend or from my spouse, will it undermine our relationship later on? If an engineer blows the whistle on misdeeds in the workplace, will it actually protect the public from harm or will it only harm the engineer's career? If we allow that apartment building to go up, will it increase traffic congestion and lower property values, or will it increase the diversity and vitality of the neighborhood and raise property values? Will the creation of a system of tradable pollution permits improve air and water quality more than would more traditional regulatory options? If we do not make concerted efforts to mitigate global climate change, will the Gulf Stream stop, plunging Europe and eastern North America into a small ice age? Might it already be too late to do anything about climate change?

All of these questions are matters of fact. They hinge on predictions about causes and effects within complex systems. The hard truth about such predictions is that our understanding of complex systems is always limited, to one degree or another, even if it is always improving. The causal connections involved are so many and so entangled one with another as to boggle the imagination, particularly when there are natural, social, and technical dynamics involved all at once. In the last section, I was able to speak with confidence about the consequences of particular projects only because the examples I gave were all either hypothetical or viewed with the benefit of hindsight, based on the naïve assumption that hindsight is always perfectly clear. When we stand at the beginnings of our projects, our view of the way into the future is usually murky enough, at least, that any conclusions we come to about what is likely to happen will be subject to reasonable dispute. As for hindsight, our view of what just happened is sometimes only slightly less murky.

For the sake of getting a handle on the problem of prediction, I would suggest an experiential model of human understanding that parallels the account of ethics in the preceding chapter. We always start trying to make sense of our experience from within particular situations, with a particular set of mental models in place about what is really going on in the world and what is likely to happen next. When other people disagree with our models or our predictions, we have many of the same options open to us as when they disagree with our moral frameworks: we can dig in our feet, clinging dogmatically to our current understanding, or we can enter into a process of inquiry.

I have already suggested that one of the most basic ways we make sense of our environment is rooted in our bodily experience: there are some things we are able to do, and some things we are not able to, and the world takes shape from there. Building on this, a simple model of inquiry would follow the metaphor of pushing and pulling. I push on my environment in a particular way, and it pushes back; I push on it in a different way, and it pushes back in a different way. As I continue to push and pull, the shape of my environment becomes more definite for me, and my expectations more precise. If I find myself in an unfamiliar place I perceive to be similar to an older and more familiar place, I anticipate the same kinds of reactions. I may be surprised, though. The place may not do what I expect, and it may do something I very much do not expect. Depending on how much attention I am paying, I may come to see that the new place is not really like the old place in some way that turns out to be relevant.

The experience of a single individual, taken on its own, may not be broad or deep enough to provide the needed refinement in discerning what is relevant and what is not in new places. So, we compare notes with one another and, through written records, with generations of people who came before us. This at least gives us a larger sample of experiences on the basis of which we can both analyze our own experiences and generalize from them. Engaging in inquiry with others has its perils, though, especially the problems of interpretation and bias.

The problem of interpretation is simply that we do not always understand one another. You may try to explain something to me, using terms both abstract and concrete, drawing pictures and pointing at things, but I still might not see what you are getting at. Your conceptual model of a particular place may be different from mine, and I simply may not have the patience or the imagination to try to see things from your point of view. Or I may assume I understand you when in fact I do not. I might then try to carry out what I think are your directions, only to be caught up short when things go badly awry. This sort of thing happens all the time.

The problem of bias is closely related to the problem of inter-pretation. I may understand what you are telling me about the world of our common experience, but I may choose to discount or ignore it because it does not jibe with some value I hold to be paramount or an ideological position to which I adhere. Or, I may suspect your advice is filtered through your own ideologi-cal position, so I mistrust what you tell me because I suspect that you may be trying to manipulate me. Does building a highway induce traffic congestion by drawing more people out onto the road, or does it just serve the pent-up demand of people who have always wanted to have just that short cut made available to them? How people answer that question may reveal as much about their attitudes and their political agendas concerning suburban development, the private automobile, and individual liberty as it does about the causes and cures of congestion.[15]

Scientific inquiry holds out the hope we can cut through all of this and achieve objective knowledge of the world. By using language more precisely and, wherever possible, expressing the regularities in the world of our experience in mathematical terms, we can avoid problems of interpretation. By subjecting all claims to rigorous scrutiny by a community of scientific inquiry, we can weed out arbitrary biases. To put this in terms of my experiential model of understanding, the sciences can be thought of as a more systematic way of pushing and pulling on our environment, usually with the help of various instruments, and developing precise, often mathematical, models that may help us to predict and explain what happens as a result. In these terms, a scientific theory is a model that is meant to explain regularities in our experience in terms of structures, entities, and forces we cannot experience directly.[16]

When a scientific theory is well established, we can generally rely on it to help organize and make sense of our ordinary experience of the world, in particular by making connections among otherwise unconnected phenomena. The emerging consensus about global climate change, for example, draws together widely dispersed activities (e.g., driving cars, raising cattle) and ties them to widely dispersed consequences (e.g., more intense storms, melting glaciers) through models of how the climate system works. Such models can help us when it comes to actually deciding what to do, since they give us a more sophisticated general understanding of which features of a given place are likely to be relevant to our projects, and they give us more precise analytical tools for distinguishing one place from another. Finally, and perhaps most importantly, models from the sciences can help us to make more confident predictions of what is likely to happen when we act.

I have been very careful here to speak only in relative terms: in many circumstances and in many ways, we may be better off with an understanding of the world that is informed by the results of scientific inquiry. This is not to say that scientific knowledge is infallible, however, or that its models should be mistaken for reality. Just as ethics should not be regarded as a set of authoritative pronouncements about what is right and good, so science should not be regarded as a set of authoritative pronouncements about what is really going on behind our experience. For one thing, the process of scientific inquiry is not finished yet, and there is good reason to doubt it ever will be. In the mean time, well-established theories may be modified or even supplanted, new connections made, new instruments developed, and so on and on. It would seem it is always too soon for scientists to start making pronouncements. Instead, they can make predictions and recommendations based on the best available theoretical models, many of which are very, very useful.[17]

More than this, the sciences are often presented as the bastion of objectivity, where assumptions, biases, and values can be weeded out of human understanding, leaving behind only hard facts. This is not entirely accurate. While the process of scientific inquiry may go a long way towards weeding out the idiosyncratic biases of individual scientists, there are still assumptions and values built into the process itself. Scientists generally prefer explanations that reduce complex wholes to the terms of their smaller parts, rather than the other way around – a reductionist bias. They prefer explanations that invoke the fewest terms – a bias towards parsimony or elegance. They prefer explanations that can be rendered mathematically over those that rely on words that can be misinterpreted – a bias towards quantifiability.

Now, it could be argued that these biases are the source of the power and usefulness of the modern sciences. There is a lot of sense in this: we have certainly been able to understand and accomplish many things through quantification and reduction. Nevertheless, there is also a lot of sense in the contention of many critics that these assumptions can too easily become a kind of ideology – reductionism or scientism – that functions as a set of authoritative pronouncements about reality. The critics charge that this ideology has systematically blinded the modern sciences to much that is of real importance in the world of our experience.[18]

There is a more modest way of stating this criticism, one that does not discount the real practical usefulness of scientific inquiry. Put simply, when we are trying to make a decision, there are relevant features of a place that should not be understood solely in scientific terms, especially those caught up in human relationships and human values. This is particularly important with regard to the social sciences, which examine human relationships and human social systems from the outside, in terms of economic exchange, desire, the broader patterns of culture, and the finer-grained patterns of biology and neurology. There is much about ourselves we can come to understand this way, and perhaps even some reasonable predictions we can make in certain circumstances and given certain assumptions. The limits of the social sciences are not just that they tend to involve more assumptions than the natural sciences, but that they study from the outside experiences and relationships we live from the inside. The scientific approach necessarily excludes many of the layers and nuances of meaning in our lived experience. This implies that a complete account of a place may include scientific accounts, but it should not be limited to them.

There are other reasons to be cautious about drawing from the sciences to inform our understanding of a place. Again, even though scientific inquiry can weed out idiosyncratic biases, there may be other biases at work besides the methodological assumptions already discussed. The sciences are a social enterprise, which human beings pursue by working together in the context of institutions that have their own particular character. Scientific research can also be expensive, requiring human labor, specialized equipment, scarce supplies, field excursions, and so on, often over long periods of time. This can have a profound influence on what scientists choose to study and the methods they can use to study it, as they are to some extent constrained to go where the money is. This ties the work of scientists directly to the interests of corporations, private foundations, and public agencies that have the money to spend. The effects of this money bias may be good or bad, but it does mean less attention will be paid to aspects of our common environment that may turn out to be important in a given instance.

Yet another reason for caution is that scientific understanding can be lost in translation, sometimes deliberately distorted when it is communicated to the broader public. One example of this is the problem of the 'hired gun'. For example, an activist or policy maker who is opposed to policies aimed at mitigating climate change might call on the expert testimony of individual scientists who do not believe climate change is really a problem. Meanwhile, an activist or policy maker in favor of those policies might call on the expert testimony of individual scientists who tend to support the more catastrophic projections of climate change. The broader public may regard the pronouncements of these dueling experts as essentially equal, cancelling one another out and providing one more demonstration of the silliness of scientists, who are always publishing conflicting studies and issuing contradictory advice.

There will always be dissenters and rogues within the scientific community, and there always should be. Dissenters perform the essential service of keeping their mainstream colleagues honest, pushing them to rethink and refine their models, re-examine their assumptions, and re-test their predictions. What will be of most genuine use to decision makers, in the long run, is what comes of that dissent when it is worked out in the field, the laboratory, and the literature, either reconfirming, modifying, or overturning the current consensus. Bringing scientific dissent directly into the public forum in order to sway public opinion amounts to an attempt to confer unearned authority on the pronouncements of a single scientist, an authority that more properly resides in the scientific community as a whole, or perhaps in the process of scientific inquiry itself.

For the sake of argument, let me set aside all of these cautions for a moment. Suppose, as in the case of climate change, there is a broad scientific consensus on the appropriate models for predicting the consequences of human actions in particular situations, and even a consensus on a range of projections and a set of recommendations for policy. Even in the best of circumstances, such projections are stated as probabilities, and they are subject to error. A particular outcome may be considered 'likely' or even 'very likely', and climate researchers have defined those terms precisely in terms of ranges of probability.[19] The essential problem is that any model of any complex system, however useful, is necessarily simpler than the system itself. Projections derived from those models may hold in general but, as the standard disclaimer says, individual results may vary.

What all of this means, when we are trying to make decisions, is that there is always much we cannot know for sure about how a project will play itself out in a given place. However observant we are, whatever the strengths of our models and the projections we derive from them, there remains the possibility of surprises, both pleasant and unpleasant. The question then becomes: How do we decide, and how do we act, in the face of irreducible uncertainty?

Notice that this is not a question that can be answered scientifically, even though the answer we give is crucial for determining how we bring scientific models and projections to bear on our understanding of particular places. It is a question that can only be answered in terms of basic attitudes about human life in the world.

Consider the more focused question of whether we should adhere to the precautionary principle. When we are faced with uncertainty in a situation in which human life and human well-being is at stake, should we err on the side of caution? That is, should we act on the assumption that we may have underestimated the dangers of what we are doing or overestimated the benefits? Or should we err on the side of confidence, in case we have overestimated the dangers and underestimated the benefits?[20] The debate sometimes seems to come down to a conflict among attitudes, from the optimism (some would say arrogance) of those who assume humans will always think of some way to triumph in the face of unpleasant surprises to the pessimism (some would say fatalism) of those who assume unpleasant surprises will overwhelm us, sooner or later.[21]

If neither of those attitudes appeals, then we can only have appeal to some other attitude. There may be any number of possibilities in between optimism and pessimism, each of which we may view as more or less reasonable, more or less practical. There is not much use in appealing to 'the facts', though, as if they could provide a neutral standpoint from which to determine whether a particular attitude is rational or not, since the whole problem came up because 'the facts' are incomplete and often selected and even shaped by human attitudes in the first place.[22]

Attitudes will have to be presented and discussed on their own terms.

In the end, though, whatever doubts remain about how the project will unfold in this place, and whatever basic attitude we have towards our prospects, we still have to choose and we still have to deal with the consequences – including the consequences of not doing anything. That much is unavoidable.

3. Metropolitan Growth

So far, I have offered a general – and, I hope, generally useful – approach to deliberation about projects in relation to the places in which they will unfold. The next step is to bring this general approach to bear on decisions within and about particular kinds of places: the specific structures and functions of metropolitan environments, especially those that have emerged as the dominant built environment of the United States. Before putting together a framework for an ethics of metropolitan growth, I should offer a guide to understanding the distinctive history and character of these particular places.

To do this, I will build on a suggestion from the last chapter, namely, that it is useful for people making decisions and pursuing projects to think of their environment as a complex system within which can be distinguished a variety of components and dynamics. In what follows, I will fill in some of the details of this model as it applies in the American metropolis, pointing out some of the natural, social, and technical dynamics that have given the built environment of the United States its distinctive character. This helps to set the scene within which people choose and pursue their projects, informing their expectations of how their projects play themselves out as well as how their projects feed back into the system, perpetuating or changing it over time.

Before I turn to that model, however, I must first attend to a matter of terminology.

3.1. How should we characterize the built environment of the United States?

It is tempting to characterize the United States as a suburban nation. By some measures, more than half of Americans now live in places that are neither in central cities nor in the rural countryside. 'Suburbia' usually serves as a catch-all term for such in-between places, however diverse they may be.[1] This sense of the term, however, is too vague to be of much use for my purposes.

In a narrower sense of the term, a suburb is a residential neighborhood of single-family houses set out on curving roads or, more recently, cul-de-sacs.[2] Houses are separated from one another by lawns and often by fences. The easiest way to get in and out of a suburb is by car, and a car may be the only way to get to work or to the store. As a consequence, commuting by car becomes a way of life. Typically, a suburb is economically and culturally dependent on the central city; in any case, commercial and industrial land uses are generally excluded from residential neighborhoods.

Suburbs in this sense began to take shape as early as the eighteenth century, as the wealthy and the cultured began setting up households in enclaves outside the central city.[3] They sought to be far enough away to avoid the problems and temptations of city life, but close enough to keep doing business there. There was precedent for this in the villas of ancient Rome and in the pastoral ideal that came to be associated with them: those who had the means could, for part of the year at least, enjoy a simpler and happier existence in the middle landscape between the city and the country. What made the new movement to the suburbs different was that it began to happen at a much larger scale, motivated in part by the industrialization of the city.

The new suburban way of life began to crystallize with the establishment, in the 1860s, of the first fully planned suburban community in the United States: Riverside, Illinois, designed by Frederick Law Olmsted and Calvert Vaux. Riverside has much in common with the great urban parks designed by Olmsted and Vaux, including New York's Central Park. Here, however, the curving roads, broad lawns, and carefully arranged greenery provided the setting for single-family houses intended for members of the emerging middle class of managers who worked in various industries in Chicago. Marketing literature for Riverside appealed explicitly to the ideal of the middle landscape:

> But Riverside is not the country, some one will say. To be sure, it is not the country, pure and simple; the country of kerosene lamps. But it is the country with the discomforts eliminated; the country *plus* city conveniences. The fortunate dweller at Riverside has plenty of fresh air and sunlight, imparting to himself and his family health and happiness. He has plenty of elbow room, and can dig to his heart's content, raise his own fruits and vegetables, keep his own cow, and even make his own butter. And he can do all this without the sacrifice of the urban comforts which long use has made a necessity to him. It is the golden mean between the two kinds of life.[4]

The outward movement of some middle-class families continued with railroad suburbs in the late nineteenth century and streetcar suburbs and early automobile suburbs in the first half of the twentieth century. It was in the period just after World War II, though, that a sea change occurred in the dynamics of American cities. William Levitt, along with his brother and father, revolutionized home-building by applying the techniques of mass production to the construction of entire neighborhoods. With the construction of the first Levittown, on Long Island, a house in the suburbs became affordable to a broader range of Americans, just as a broader range of Americans aspired to a house in the suburbs. Urban critics scoffed, but people moved to Levittown and its descendants in droves.

At the beginning of the twenty-first century there are still many people living in places that can be characterized as suburban in this sense, but more and more are living and working in places that are not really urban or rural, but not really suburban either.

At least since the middle of the twentieth century, commercial and industrial development has followed residential development out of the city, while supposedly suburban patterns of development have made their way in towards the center.[5] As a consequence, instead of the stereotypical pattern of residential suburbs surrounding central cities, an entirely different kind of metropolis has been emerging. It could well be said that the United States has entered a post-suburban era.

In sum, 'suburb' is either too vague or too narrow to serve as an accurate description of the places where most Americans live and work. A further problem is that the term is bound up with stereotypes and pre-packaged value judgments. For many of those who move there, a suburban neighborhood still seems to be a refuge in an idyllic middle landscape, away from the city with its many problems and dangers. It is a place to have some access to nature – but not too much. It is a safe and healthy place to raise children, and a safe place to build wealth in the value of real estate. To early critics, however, a suburb was the very symbol of stultifying conformity, the superficiality of middle-class values, and the aesthetic boredom of tacky little boxes. To more recent critics, a suburbs stands for all of this – though the boxes may now be larger – but also for social injustice and ecological unsustainability besides.

'Sprawl' is the most common alternative to 'suburb' as a term for the typical American landscape. While the term may have originated with critics of the ways in which American metropolitan areas expand, 'sprawl' has since entered into everyday language. In common usage, the term has the advantage that it can encompass many different kinds of metropolitan landscape, not just traditional suburbs. The common thread that runs through these landscapes is that they are caught up in a specific process by which metropolitan areas spread out into the surrounding countryside. There is a curious ambiguity in the term, though, as 'sprawl' can stand for both the process and the product of expansion.

There have been a number of attempts to develop a useful and rigorous definition of 'sprawl', both as process and as product.[6] In common usage, however, 'sprawl' seems to function as a handy catch-all term for those parts of the metropolis people dislike. Metaphorically, sprawl suggests that the city has collapsed, like a drunkard on a sidewalk, and is now spreading inexorably outwards, oblivious to the surrounding countryside. Development intrudes into rural and wild landscapes like the sharp elbow and kicking heel of a rude bedfellow, pushing aside or simply crushing everything in its path. In the eyes of activists sprawl is so bad that the definition of the term needs be little more than a catalogue of the damage done: according to literature from the Sierra Club, for example, 'suburban sprawl is irresponsible, poorly planned development that destroys green space, increases traffic and air pollution, crowds schools and drives up taxes'.[7] From time to time, the word is itself used to name some of the bad effects of the expanding metropolis: it is not just that sprawling development turns out to be ugly, but that 'sprawl' is itself a synonym for 'ugliness'.

These strong negative connotations give good reason to avoid using the term 'sprawl'. The goal of the ethics of the built environment is to make thoughtful judgments and responsible decisions within and about the places where we live. In a complex metropolitan fabric shaped by a complex process of growth, there is likely to be much that is good alongside much that is bad – and in any case there is likely to be sharp disagreement about which is which. The language we use to describe the landscape should, as much as possible, leave open the question of whether and in what respects the landscape is good or bad. To talk about the built environment of the United States as 'sprawl', or even as 'suburban', is too often to pass judgment on it without really thinking at all.

The term, 'metropolitan growth', has several advantages over both 'suburb' and 'sprawl'. True, it does not flow very easily from the tongue, and there are several other problems with the term, but I think these shortcomings are at least manageable.

'Growth' has the advantage of drawing attention to the dynamic character of landscapes. The most interesting and urgent ethical questions arise as landscapes change from one configuration to another as part of the process by which development expands and intensifies. A process may be thought of as moving towards some particular goal. In principle, at least, a process can be redirected towards some new goal, perhaps even as the result of conscious choices based on careful deliberation. Particular land-use practices and policies are often concerned precisely with shaping dynamic processes, allowing and encouraging some kinds of change while forbidding or discouraging others.

'Metropolitan' is preferable to 'suburban' because it is broad enough to tie together diverse landscapes in and around cities, leaving open the possibility of drawing finer distinctions as needed. Post-war suburban subdivisions are certainly a significant part of the metropolitan fabric, but so are nineteenth-century Romantic enclaves, scattered exurban houses, older town centers that have been absorbed into the fabric, edge cities, industrial parks, mega-malls, and so on. Each type of landscape can be distinguished from the others by its own particular history, woven into the broader history of the region.

Perhaps the greatest advantage of 'metropolitan growth' is that it is at least closer than 'sprawl' to being ethically neutral – though not entirely so. Metaphorically, 'growth' is intertwined with value judgments, but these judgments can cut both ways. Growth can be good, like the development of a child towards maturity; in this sense, the term implies progress towards perfection. Commentators often seem to regard both metropolitan expansion and economic growth as inherently good, taking them to be indicators of general human progress: a continuing rise in median home values and in the number of housing starts means our children will be better off than we are. Growth can also be bad, like the development of a tumor, bringing with it the horror of impending death. This is the metaphor of choice for some critics of metropolitan growth, who equate expanding development with the spread of a peculiar kind of cancer across the landscape.

My hope for the term rests on the possibility of playing these metaphors off against one another, balancing or cancelling out some of the built-in prejudices. At the very least, I think I can plausibly insist on using the term 'growth' in a much more neutral sense, simply to designate an increase in both the surface area and the intensity of development in a metropolitan area. I take it as fairly uncontroversial that cities in the United States (and elsewhere) have tended to grow and that, as a consequence, landscapes in and around cities have changed and continue to change. As far as I am concerned, it has yet to be decided whether this expansion is good or bad, and whether it is inevitable.

Though I do not really need to do so for my purposes here, my off-the-cuff definition of 'growth' suggests how it might be possible to operationalize the term. One important dimension of growth is the simple increase in the area of land that is developed or set aside for particular kinds of non-agricultural uses, including urban parks. Another is the increase in the intensity of development, by some measure: perhaps the percentage of the area covered by impermeable surfaces. Metropolitan growth is also intertwined with other measures of growth that have some bearing on decision making. These include growth in population, number of households, automobile use, economic activity, tax revenues, the costs of infrastructure and basic services, and so on.

An alternative to 'metropolitan growth' deserves some consideration: 'metropolitan change'. There is no rule that says all metropolitan areas have to grow and, even when they do, growth within metropolitan areas does not happen everywhere all the time. From the point of view of a particular decision maker, the most pressing problems may arise from a decline in development, population, or opportunity. Historically, this has been the experience of many in rural towns and inner cities, living in the midst of local retreat and decline within the larger context of

growth. 'Metropolitan change' still captures the ethical signifi-
cance of changing landscapes, without suggesting that everyone
is dealing with growth all the time.

There are still good reasons to prefer 'metropolitan growth'.
For one thing, 'metropolitan change' moves away from the distinctive features of most American metropolitan areas through
recent history and closer to the more general heading of the
ethics of the built environment. Since I am mostly interested in
decisions people face in the context of particular landscapes in
the United States, 'metropolitan growth' seems to be a better fit.
Even if growth is temporarily stalled, there seems to be a broad
consensus that restarting it should be a high national priority. The
number of new houses under construction at any given time is
still widely cited as a key measure of economic health: the more
the better.

As for the observation that growth does not occur everywhere
at once, 'metropolitan growth' can still apply to areas that are
stable or in decline if they are part of an overall pattern or system
of growth in the metropolis as a whole, as populations and economic investment shift from one area to another. For example,
the depopulation of rural areas far away from cities is caught up in
the dynamics of metropolitan growth, driven by broader patterns
of shifting economic opportunity, shifting population, changing
technology, and so on.

3.2. What are the dynamics that shape the built environment?

Until the recent slowdown, metropolitan growth had been going
on all over the world, in one form or another. If there is anything
that distinguishes the American style of growth from other styles,
it is most likely to be found by looking carefully at the processes of
growth that are peculiar to the United States. If American metropolitan areas are the result of a unique confluence of causes, then

they are likely to offer a distinctive backdrop for the decisions and projects of everyday life.

Attempts to explain the American landscape in terms of a single cause – the automobile, for example, or particular government regulations – are generally not very satisfying. Each seems to account for some features of the landscape, but not for others. A transportation system based almost entirely on the private automobile certainly has a lot of influence on patterns of development, if only because we keep having to build roads so we have places to drive them, and parking lots and garages so we have places to store them. However, traditional suburbs had their start and perhaps even reached their peak before the automobile came on the scene. There is something of a chicken-and-egg problem here: did people start moving away from the central city because they suddenly had cars available to them, or did they start buying cars because they wanted, for other reasons, to move away from the central city? It seems likely that it was a little of both, and that various motivations and causes are all bound up together.

This is the point at which it becomes useful for decision makers within metropolitan areas to think of their environment as a system or overlapping set of systems, with causes and effects bound up together in a complex web. A change in one part of the system can set off a cascade of effects through the whole system, with various feedbacks that may reinforce or suppress the causes of the initial change. For the purposes of explanation, thinking of a metropolis as a system implies that a single cause or a single effect cannot be fully understood in isolation from other causes and effects. So, while it may be useful to analyze the system into its various components – transportation technology, for example, or cultural values – in the end we have to find some way of considering those components and their interactions all at once.

To be more specific, a metropolis may qualify as a technological system or, more properly, a socio-technical ensemble.[8] This means some very important components of the system consist of technical hardware: automobiles, roads, bridges, gas stations, water pipes, sewers, power plants, cell phone towers, and the like. Hardware does not make much sense apart from the social components of the system that at least in part determine what the hardware means, what it is for, and how it is to be used. Public institutions, private corporations, markets, laws, and regulations are among the social components of the system, but so are ideas, values, and social mores.

A metropolis has its roots in the most basic technological activity of altering the natural environment to support particular human projects. We cannot live very well in raw wilderness without at least a few implements for gathering food and keeping warm. Human settlements are larger and more complex implements for meeting these goals, and others besides. But the built environments in which we live are alterations of the natural environment, not substitutes for it. Like other implements, to establish a village or a city is to rearrange or redirect natural processes. We encourage and amplify processes we find helpful, like the flow of water or the growth of certain grasses. We deflect or suppress those we find harmful, like the free movement of large predators or the fall of rain toward our beds. Perhaps more than other technological systems, the built environment remains rooted in and intertwined with the natural world, so natural processes continue to play an important role in giving it shape.

Also, more than other technological devices or systems, a metropolis is not the creation of a single designer with a single intention. If anything, it is a system that has emerged over time from the efforts of many different people pursuing different projects for different reasons. The system does not have just one purpose or just one meaning, and it may not respond readily to the efforts of one individual or group to change or direct it. As a system, a metropolis is more like a hurricane than like a mammal or an airplane, in the sense that organization is relatively loose and it does not have a central control system.

(a) Natural dynamics

Some of the distinctiveness of the American metropolis will be found in the natural dynamics that underlie it. The United States is big. There is a lot of land available for settlement, much of which is good for growing crops and raising livestock. Though it varies from west to east, there is generally some source of water available for drinking, irrigation, and transportation. The climate is generally temperate, though this varies from south to north. Some places have particularly harsh winters while others have oppressive summers; a few places seem to have both. The wind generally blows from west to east and water always flows downhill, which affect the flow of wastes produced by human settlements. This creates upstream/downstream relationships between places.

Particular landforms also have an influence. The cities of the East Coast with their natural harbors, peninsulas and islands will be somewhat different from cities of the Great Plains with their wide, flat spaces and from Los Angeles settled in its valley. Elevation may also make a difference. Cities on the coast, lying near or below sea level, have to adapt to different conditions from cities at higher elevation, in or near mountains.

It should also be said that there are natural forces at work in humans. It is because we are animals of a certain type, with certain natural capacities and limitations, that we rearrange our environment to begin with. Aside from metabolism, with its demand for food and water, we have other drives or instincts that arise from our origins as social mammals: we tend to live together, to cooperate or compete with one another, and perhaps to seek the approval of our peers. One particular feature of our lives as animals relates directly to metropolitan growth: natural population increase, though the particular ways in which we find mates and raise children is at least as much a matter of culture as of nature.

(b) Social dynamics

Cultural heritage looms large among the social dynamics that shape metropolitan growth. American patterns of land use reflect the importance of the idea of private property in American culture, the ideal of owning land and a house, protecting it, and building wealth from it. Here, the mere physical fact that America is big takes on a particular meaning: all of this land is potential real estate, and the sheer size of the continent means that, however much one person may acquire, there is still always some left for others. This is very different from the meaning of the land for the tribes that lived in it before the arrival of European explorers and settlers.

There are other, more particular, cultural values in play as well. One of these has already been mentioned: the pastoral ideal of the middle landscape. While pastoralism has roots that go back at least to ancient Rome, it has had its most profound impact on American life through the Romantic movement in art and the English picturesque tradition in landscape design. Olmsted and Vaux drew from these sources in their designs for the urban parks for which they are best known, and also in their design for Riverside.[9] When suburban living became more widely available after World War II, the whole of the expanding middle class could aspire to living in an attractive neighborhood of houses in a park, with curving roads and broad lawns, away from the city with its grid of streets, its noise, and its filth.

The pursuit of cultural values and individual desires is given further shape by the dynamics of markets, including markets for real estate and for the various goods and services that make it possible to build, maintain, and inhabit places within the metropolis. To some extent, at least, the choices people make about where and how to build and to live are constrained by what is available for purchase. Sometimes, an economic mechanism takes on a life of its own, merging with deeply held cultural values. This is the case with the process of subdivision, which is simply the trick of buying a large piece of land, dividing it up, and selling off parcels one at a time. With the rise of the post-war suburb, the noun 'sub-division' became almost synonymous with 'neighborhood'.

An important feature of economic activity in the United States is the emergence of a mass market: producers have been able to advertise and sell their products from coast to coast, reaching potential consumers through mass media. Not only does this mean that many of the same goods and services are available everywhere, but that people everywhere begin to want more of the same goods and services. Advertisers have been able to project and reinforce images of the good life that are not tied to particular places, creating a consumer culture that may serve to dilute local and regional differences. A subdivision or a strip mall in the Pacific Northwest is very much like a subdivision or a strip mall in the Southeast, whatever other differences there may be between the two regions.

For their part, markets are shaped and constrained by public institutions and laws, another important part of the social dynamics of the American metropolis. A founding idea of the United States is that the central function of government is to protect private property and to set and enforce the rules for market transactions. These rules often set up incentives and disincentives that have a direct impact on the choices made by individuals. In tax policy, to take just one example, the long-standing deduction for mortgage interest payments is an incentive, not only to own a home, but to trade up to larger and more expensive homes. Governments at various levels have also played an important role in building and maintaining the physical infrastructure that makes economic activity possible, but sometimes in a way that pushes the shape of that infrastructure in a particular direction. Since the beginning of the twentieth century, for example, public spending on transportation has shown a distinct bias towards the private automobile and away from passenger rail.[10]

Public institutions also play a role in protecting people from harm, including nuisances. Building codes and licensing procedures for construction trades have been put in place to protect people from illness, injury, and death as well as from fraud. At the same time, occupational safety regulations have been put in place to protect those who are actually involved in construction. Some environmental regulations are an extension of this function of government, aiming to ensure that people are not exposed to toxic substances in the air they breathe or the water they drink, and that they are not subjected to excessive noise or to terribly ugly things. In the United States, though, the public institution that may have had the most profound impact on the process of metropolitan growth is the zoning board.

The original idea of zoning, as it emerged in the 1920s, is that some land uses are too dangerous or too unpleasant to be allowed near places where people actually live. So, all of the industrial slaughterhouses, to take just one example, would be confined to a particular district that is set apart from the rest of the city. Within a few decades, this idea developed into what is sometimes called Euclidean zoning, with a strict separation of uses: residential zones must exclude all commercial and industrial uses, commercial zones must exclude all residential and industrial uses, and so on. The result is a landscape of patches and pods connected together by long, busy roads.

Another function governments have played in the United States, though less so than elsewhere, is to help people who are in need. There have been various efforts to provide public housing and to renew urban centers that were left behind by growth. These efforts have sometimes met with success, perhaps more often not.[11] In any case, they have had a direct influence on the shape of the built environment, if only through the demolition of old urban neighborhoods and the construction of housing projects.

This brings up other important social dynamics in the United States: the population of the United States is diverse, and that diversity has often given rise to tension and conflict. Prejudices that run along the lines of race and culture became the basis for a separate form of zoning. Instead of excluding noxious or dangerous land uses, though, this parallel zoning excluded people who were perceived as unacceptably different. Early suburbs were strictly segregated by race, class, and even religion: in its early years, the first Levittown explicitly excluded blacks and Jews.

While patterns of segregation may have arisen on their own, racial prejudices were also institutionalized, and not only in the South. With the New Deal, the Federal Housing Administration (FHA) started to guarantee home mortgages in order to encourage banks to lend money to potential home-owners. The FHA would not guarantee all mortgages, however, as some loans were considered too risky. So-called Residential Security Maps, developed by another agency, marked particularly high-risk neighborhoods in red, which gave the name of 'redlining' to the policy of denying federal guarantees to mortgages in those neighborhoods. The presence of even one black family in a neighborhood was considered enough for that neighborhood to be regarded as an unacceptable risk.[12]

The practice of redlining officially ended in the mid 1970s, and even traditional suburbs have become more diverse, but patterns of segregation have left their marks in the landscape. There are monuments to the past here and there, including a concrete wall built between two neighborhoods near Detroit so the all-white neighborhood on one side of the wall could qualify for FHA guarantees.[13] More significantly, each metropolitan area still has a distinct racial and ethnic geography: some areas are widely understood to be predominantly white, others predominantly black, and yet others predominantly Latino, with concentrations of other ethnic groups in pockets here and there.[14]

There is also a widespread form of segregation by economic class. New subdivisions in the United States have generally been built so the houses all fall within a relatively narrow price range. This means people who are looking to buy a new house will sort themselves by how much they can afford, which means they will end up living near others who make about the same amount of money they do, often in similar lines of work. The uniformity of property values – and of neighbors – is often perceived as a guarantee of the stability of property values. Not all economic segregation occurs on the periphery: there are exclusive older neighborhoods, and an influx of more affluent people into a relatively disadvantaged neighborhood can drive up property values and drive out less affluent residents.

(c) Technological dynamics

Natural and cultural dynamics are intertwined with technological dynamics, by which I mean not only technical devices but also techniques, that is, the know-how and the methods for getting things done.

There is, of course, the technology involved in the construction of buildings themselves. The wood-frame house that became the standard for American suburbs depends on the availability of machine nails and pre-cut lumber, innovations of the nineteenth century, as well as modern power tools and heavy machinery. As already noted, William Levitt's real breakthrough in the late 1940s was to apply techniques of mass production to the construction of a residential neighborhood. The process of building a house was broken down into a series of discrete tasks, then teams of workers would move from lot to lot, each performing its single task and moving on.[15]

There are also the technological devices involved in running a household, many of which are now generally taken for granted: running hot and cold water, electric lighting, central heating and air conditioning, electronic thermostats, refrigerators, stoves and ovens, automatic dishwashers, laundry machines, trash compactors, vacuum cleaners, and any number of others. One set of devices in particular has had a profound impact on the American landscape: lawn-care equipment. It was with the invention of the push lawnmower in the late nineteenth century that, for the first time, one person working alone could realize the ideal of the picturesque tradition: a close-cut lawn of green grass as the appropriate setting for a home.

The relationships among different parts of the landscape have been shaped by transportation and communication technology. Older metropolitan areas, like Boston or New York, still have some patterns carried over from the past: the density and compactness of walking cities, the early rings and tendrils of neighborhoods served by horse cars and streetcars, the old suburban towns served by commuter rail, and the far-flung developments served by private automobiles on public roads. Observers have noted that these different technologies have different tendencies: railroads tend to draw in development, creating dense and busy clusters around stations, while automobiles tend to spread development out, if only because drivers need places to park.

Communication infrastructure also runs through the landscape, from telegraph and telephone lines to fiber-optic cable and cell towers. It seems likely that the ability to communicate easily across distances will have a significant influence on how people use and move around the landscape. It may (or may not) be easier and more satisfying to shop online than drive to the mall, or to hold a video conference rather than fly to a meeting in another city. In any case, people now have a wider (or at least different) array of options for going about the business of life than did people in the past.

The devices and techniques of mass communication are also important factors in the emergence of mass culture. With radio and television, advertisers could instantly reach a national audience, and have done so with increasing sophistication. As those technologies have matured, and as other electronic media have developed, advertisers have also been able to target narrower audiences with their messages, focusing on those most likely to buy what they have to sell.

(d) Interactions

So far, I have done little more than list some of the components of the metropolitan system as it has emerged in the United States. There have already been some hints as to how some parts of the system interact with others, but it is worth looking a little more closely at one example before moving on. Note that this example is simplified, focusing only on a small set of interactions rather than on the system as a whole; there are any number of complicating factors I will leave out for the sake of illustration.

The reaction of many Americans to the industrial city is part of a positive feedback loop among the natural, social, and technical components of the metropolitan system. The process of industrialization was both technical and social. It involved the development of new techniques and new machines, of course, but it was rooted in particular ways of thinking about the natural world, human ingenuity, property, prosperity, and progress, and it was supported by markets and by government incentives. As economic activity shifted towards new industries, more and more people made their way into the cities, from rural areas and from overseas, in the hope of finding and keeping jobs. They lived as close as they could to the factories, packed into the tenement slums that became, for many Americans, the symbol of the industrial city.

People living in tenements suffered from the natural consequences of overcrowding, restricted flows of air and water, and the life cycles of various pathogens: stress, filth, and disease. These conditions supported the cultural stigma that already applied to the poor and the foreign in the eyes of white, middle- and upper-class Americans. The culture of the more affluent classes also presented them with an alternative, the pastoral middle landscape, which was made available to them by transportation, construction, and lawn-care technology, by the natural systems and open land at the periphery of the metropolis, and by economic and legal systems that enabled and encouraged home ownership. The cultural ideal was also useful as a marketing tool for developers.

As more people were able to move out of the city, they took their investment power and potential to generate tax revenue with them. Poor and minority populations were left behind, excluded from the suburbs by housing prices or by explicit discrimination. Conditions in the central city deteriorated, with higher concentrations of poverty and declines in economic opportunity and in the ability of city governments to provide basic services. As a consequence, central cities came more and more to resemble the cultural stereotype that motivated people to leave in the first place. Even now, when many central cities in the United States have revived or are reviving, many people who live in outlying parts of the metropolis can sometimes react to the idea of living in the city as though it were still a hive of tenement slums, filthy, dangerous, and corrupt.

Other examples of interaction among the various components of the metropolitan system will arise later on, as will some factors that complicate the story I have just told. My goal here has been simply to illustrate the ways in which the interactions of various dynamics can give a built environment its distinctive character.

Before moving on, I should note that the systems approach to understanding the built environment can apply at different scales. For example, I have been speaking of American metropolitan areas as though they make up a single, coherent group, despite the apparent differences between Boston and Los Angeles, for example, or Atlanta and Seattle. American metropolitan areas do have a great deal in common because many of the dynamics that shape them are at work everywhere across the country, from federal policy to cultural ideas promulgated through mass media and mass marketing. They may nonetheless differ from one another to the extent those national-scale dynamics interact with more local dynamics, perhaps especially the peculiarities of local culture and history as they interact with local natural conditions.

4. The Ethics of Metropolitan Growth

Individuals and groups trying to make decisions about their environment and how to live in it need a clear understanding of what is at stake. Some such decisions are especially difficult because there is quite a lot at stake on all sides: any given option preserves some values and destroys others, meets some obligations and violates others.

The framework in Table 4.1 is intended as a tool to help decision makers sort through the complexity of many important decisions regarding the built environment, to identify the values and obligations that may be at stake in a given situation.[1] The framework is organized into four main parts, each of which is defined by an ethical question. The parts are further divided into more specific factors or issues that may play into a particular decision.

Well-being concerns the degree to which a given place makes it possible for the people who live there to flourish, not just as a matter of physical health but also mental health and personal development. This part of the framework is most closely tied to the ancient philosophical tradition for which the main question of ethics is: What is the best kind of life for a human being? The variation here is: What kind of place makes it possible for people to live the best kind of life?

Not everyone benefits equally from good places, however, and not everyone pays an equal share of the costs of creating and maintaining them. This raises questions of *justice* or, more broadly, questions about our obligations to help and not to harm

Table 4.1

Ethics in the Built Environment	

WELL-BEING
Is this a good place to live?

Health	Family Life
Safety	Recreation
Economic Opportunity	Mobility
Educational Opportunity	Aesthetics
Cultural Opportunity	Security
Community	

JUSTICE
Who gets to benefit from this place, and who does not?

Community	Marital/Family Status
Class	Physical Ability
Race	Other Species
Sex/Gender	Other Generations

SUSTAINABILITY
How long can this place last?

Economic Sustainability
Cultural Sustainability
Ecological Sustainability

LEGITIMACY
Who should make decisions about this place?

Property	Transparency
Citizen Involvement	Leadership
Coordination	

one another. In the built environment, justice often arises as an issue of access to the opportunity to pursue a good life. If people have succeeded in securing a good life in a good place, what obligations do they have, if any, to ensure that others can also secure a good life in a good place? At minimum, what obligations do they have, if any, to ensure that others are not actually harmed as a result of their way of living? On what grounds, if any, can particular individuals and groups be excluded from particular places?

To ask whether a place is *sustainable* is to ask how long people can go on living good lives there given the constraints imposed by the broader context. In the long run, could living an otherwise good life in this place be a self-defeating project? Some of the conditions for sustaining particular places and particular ways of living are ecological, but there are also economic and cultural conditions that should be taken into account.

Finally, there are questions about the *legitimacy* of the decision-making process itself, questions that stand on the border between ethics and politics. Who has the right and the authority to make this kind of decision about this place or about how to live within it? Some decisions may best be left to individuals while others call for some sort of collective decision making or delegation to one political authority or other – and there is likely to be heated debate about which is which. In the built environment of the United States, questions of jurisdiction and scale are especially pressing: Should this decision be made at the level of the household, the neighborhood, the city, the county, the region, the state, or the federal government?

The framework is not intended as a set of rules, or as an algorithm for producing good decisions, or as a way of keeping score. It is intended as a comprehensive set of questions to be asked that can help to frame the decision that is to be made. People trying to make a decision together may disagree about what each question in the framework means and whether the question is relevant to the decision at hand. Even if they are in agreement on the questions, they may still disagree in the answers they give. Using this framework, though, they may at least arrive at a clearer and more precise understanding of where they disagree and what work they still have to do in order to make a decision.

4.1. Is this a good place to live? (Well-being)

A particular place offers a particular set of opportunities to pursue projects, and imposes a particular set of constraints. Some projects are more central than others to human survival and human flourishing. There is likely to be little debate that securing clean drinking water and adequate food are vital human projects, and that a place is good to the extent it makes it possible to pursue those projects.

Beyond the basics of survival, though, there is likely to be disagreement about what makes a good place to live because there is disagreement about what makes a good human life. What opportunities do we really need in order to flourish? What constraints should we try to avoid, and which should we embrace because they help to keep us out of trouble? Access to adequate food may be essential to a good human life, but access to the food court of a modern shopping mall, someone could argue, may be downright harmful.

(a) Health

Some places are better than others in helping people to stay healthy. This is most obvious when a place poses a direct threat to the living, functioning or normal development of an individual. Love Canal, a neighborhood in Niagara Falls, New York, that was built atop a toxic waste dump, turned out to be a very bad place to live, perhaps especially for children. The tenements of early industrial cities in the United States were also very bad places to live, with too many people and not enough sewers. By contrast, much of the appeal of suburban development for those who could afford to move there has been the prospect of cleaner air and water and better sanitation in a place removed from the (real and imagined) pollution and disease of the industrial city.

There are also matters of public health that may not be as obvious as matters of individual health. From my own point of view as an individual, sanitation is good because it protects me from disease. From the point of view of public health, sanitation is good because it reduces the incidence of disease across a whole population. The public health perspective is useful because it can reveal unexpected patterns of health and illness linked to structures in the built environment. For example, some preliminary research has suggested that a transportation system based on the private automobile is linked to a rising rate of obesity in the United States, which is linked in turn to rates of heart disease, diabetes, and other health problems.[2] The causal connection is supposed to be that walking is no longer a regular part of everyday life: the various parts of the metropolitan environment people use every day are located far apart from one another, and roads are laid out in a way that makes it difficult or dangerous to walk or ride a bike from one place to another. The result is a decrease in physical activity and a rise in the rate of obesity.

Mental health is also a concern. Some places may be inherently stressful or alienating while other places may better support the development of balanced and well-adjusted people. There is likely to be sharp disagreement about which is which, especially along the cultural fault-line between city and suburb: viewed from each side, life on the other side seems dangerously out of balance, leading to anxiety, neurosis, and various other pathological states. More seriously, there are places about which there is less likely to be disagreement: parts of the inner cities or small rural towns that have been damaged by isolation, abandonment, and discrimination seem to expose people living in them to greater risks of both physical and mental illness.

(b) Safety

Safety from bodily injury and property damage is also of value to people. The possible causes of injury and property damage may be deliberate or accidental, and they may involve other humans, animals, technological devices (including cars), buildings, infrastructure, or natural forces. All else being equal, places are better than others if they have lower crime rates, more stable buildings with better fire escape plans, better traffic signals, better crosswalks and more considerate drivers, fewer abandoned wells, a lower likelihood of flooding, and so on.

No place can be perfectly safe, though, and people have to tolerate a certain level of risk in order to pursue the projects that make up a good life. The question then is: Which risks are acceptable, and which are not? It appears many Americans are willing to accept a significant risk of death or injury in automobile accidents, for example, but expect a very low risk of injury or property loss from crime. Part of the reason for this is that people are more willing to tolerate a risk they have consented to (driving) than a risk imposed on them from outside (crime).[3] Still, there is considerable room for debate on the question of how safe we want to be and at what cost.

A wrinkle in the question of safety is that perception is sometimes more important to people than the underlying reality: we often want to *feel* more safe even if, statistically speaking, we are not *in fact* more safe. Perception of risk can be influenced by prejudice and fear of difference. So, people may feel endangered when they find themselves in places unlike those they are used to and confronted by people who are unlike themselves in some way they perceive as relevant, even if the risk of harm is actually very low. They may also overlook actual risks in more familiar surroundings.

(c) Economic opportunity

People need various material things (goods) in order to sustain life: water, food, clothing, shelter and so on. Beyond subsistence, they need material things and often the help of other people (services) in order to pursue the various projects they see as contributing to a good life. Individuals on their own are seldom able to produce all of the goods they need, so they enter into exchanges and other kinds of agreements with others. Stripped down to its essence, then, economic opportunity is the chance to participate in exchanges with others to acquire goods and services. Economic relationships in contemporary America may look much more complicated than this, but the underlying logic of exchange remains fairly simple.

Living in a particular place may make it more or less easy for people to earn a living, to buy things they need and things they want, to borrow money for special purposes, to save and invest money for the future, and perhaps even to accumulate some degree of wealth. If economic activity shifts from one place to another – from small towns to big cities, for example, from central cities to outer suburbs – people may find themselves stuck with very little economic opportunity, and perhaps a slimmer chance of living a good life. Jobs may be scarce, as may be banks willing to lend money and stores to sell certain kinds of goods. Housing costs may be too high for people to buy or rent adequate shelter, or property values may be too stagnant for the purposes of investment.

At a broader scale, places may be evaluated on conditions in the broader natural, cultural, and political environment that support or thwart economic activity. This may include access to sources of energy and raw materials, fertile soil and a favorable climate for growing food, a landscape or seascape that makes transporta-tion easier, and so on. The political environment may do well or poorly at sustaining markets and upholding agreements between people, and there may be incentives in place that push economic activity in one direction or another. For example, the mortgage interest tax deduction in the United States has proven to be a strong incentive towards home ownership among Americans, and perhaps an important driver of metropolitan growth.

Note that economic opportunity is just one component of what makes a good place: it may be impossible to live a good life without it, but having it does not guarantee a good life. In techni-cal terms, economic opportunity is a necessary condition but not a sufficient condition for a good life; other values must be taken into account as well. People in the contemporary world need work, but may be right to insist on work that is meaningful and satisfying to them; they need to consume goods and services, but not just any goods and services will do.

(d) Educational opportunity

Education serves at least two purposes. It is often thought of as the key that opens up greater economic opportunity, including a chance to leave places where opportunities are scarce. Much discussion about the quality of public education in the United States focuses on the competitiveness of graduates compared to graduates in other places or graduates of earlier generations. Families trying to decide where to live will often look first at the public school system and perhaps nearby private schools, asking themselves how likely each school would be to prepare their children for economic success.

People also look to education for knowledge and skills of no immediate economic value. Through education, people may try to expand their understanding of the world and of their own history, learn basic values and develop character, acquire healthy habits, foster and discipline their own creativity, and become responsible and well-rounded citizens. Not all of these goals can be met through formal education, and there is actually serious debate as to whether some of them should be. This suggests that educational opportunity includes access to resources for self-improvement outside of formal schooling: libraries, public lectures, discussion groups, music lessons, dance lessons, martial arts instruction, nature centers, book clubs, religious instruction, and so on.

(e) Cultural opportunity

The core meaning of 'culture', as I use it here, is a set of traditions that has developed among a particular group of people in a particular place, including everything from mores and religious beliefs to language and story-telling to food, dress and dance.

One take on cultural opportunity is the chance for people to learn their own heritage as members of particular ethnic or religious groups. This may be closely allied with the second, broader sense of education, if developing a sense of identity is understood as part of overall self-improvement. From this perspective, a good place allows regular contact with the cultural traditions of one's own group, and offers some protection of those traditions from disruptive influences, including what some see as the bland commercialism of American popular culture. European immigrants to the United States in the late nineteenth and early twentieth century tended at first to settle in ethnic enclaves, surrounded by people with the same heritage. So it is with many Latino communities today, with cultural resources expanded to include Spanish-language broadcasting and a controversial trend towards bilingualism in commerce and in government services. Conventional suburbs have sometimes been taken as enclaves for the protection of middle-class American values and customs.

A very different take on cultural opportunity is the pull towards assimilation and cosmopolitanism, turning away from the constraints of particular traditions towards the idea that each individual is a citizen of the world. From this point of view, a place offers cultural opportunity if it allows people to experience many different cultures, in part for purposes of education but also just to add some variety to life. So, it may be good to be able to learn other languages and to learn how others experience and think about the world in order to put one's own language, experience, and thoughts in perspective; it may even allow a critical perspective on cultural traditions as such. At the same time, it may simply be enjoyable to try food from different cultures, to see costume and dance, to hear songs, and the like. All of this places some value on access to ethnic neighborhoods, festivals and restaurants.

The western European roots of mainstream American culture still show in the value many Americans place on exposure to European high culture: an art museum, a symphony orchestra, a ballet company, an opera house, a theatre company, a

Shakespeare festival, a formal garden. Even the suburban pattern of development has been influenced by a particular expression of English high culture, the picturesque movement in landscape design.

(f) Family life

There is room for disagreement about what a family is or may be. The traditional American model consists of a husband and wife living in a detached, single-family home with their children. The percentage of American households that fit the traditional model has been declining, though, and is likely to continue to decline.[4] Meanwhile, alternatives clamor for attention: childless couples, single parents, same-sex couples with or without children, and households that include members of extended families.

Whatever the model, part of the value of a place is the degree to which it supports family life. It may be easier or harder to find housing suitable for a particular family, to arrange for the care of young children, to live near other relatives, and to adapt the household to include aging parents or other members of the extended family. Particular places and their demands may put serious strain on the partnership between parents in a household, as when one parent remains isolated at home while the other goes to work, or when both parents commute to work in different directions with few options for childcare in between.

Many of the concerns of family life focus on children, who do have particular needs beyond the basics of health, safety, and education. Children need the opportunity to play with other children, to interact with adult role models, and to participate in activities that aid their development. Conventional American suburbs are still widely perceived as good places to raise children precisely for these reasons, especially newly built suburbs in which the adult residents are more or less in the same stage of life. As children get older, though, their needs change so being in a neighborhood with other children may no longer be enough for them: access to other kinds of engaging activities may become more important, and perhaps harder to attain.[5]

(g) Recreation

Children need places to play, and adults may need them as well. So, all else being equal, a place that provides opportunities for leisure activities of various kinds may be better than one that does not. These can include a public park, a bowling alley, a gym, a baseball diamond or soccer field with or without organized teams, a climbing wall, a large backyard, a lake for water sports, a river for fishing, a bicycle path, a forest for hiking and hunting, and so on. Recently, in the United States, whole residential sub-divisions have been built with leisure in mind, with tennis courts, swimming pools, or even golf courses at their hearts.

The value of recreation is closely tied to the value of health. Since physical activity is no longer a part of everyday life for most Americans, their health depends more on what they do in their time off. Recreation is also thought of as having benefits for mental health, releasing the stress of a hectic work week by playing hard on the weekend, or perhaps leaving behind the noise of modern life for a walk in the woods.

Some of the value of 'green space' lies here. At least since the days of John Muir, many Americans have believed that regular contact with nature – or at least with less-built environments – is necessary for refreshing the soul even as physical activity in nature is necessary for strengthening the body.

(h) Mobility

In order to take advantage of the various opportunities in the built environment, people have to be able to get to them. Most basi-cally, people need some means of transportation and corridors through which to travel. Walking is the oldest and most basic means of transportation, and cities used to be built so all of their various functions were within walking distance of one another. Americans are now mostly dependent on private automobiles and public roads, with the various functions of the built environment separated from one another and spread out over great distances. In some circumstances, Americans may have other options: bicycles, buses, trolleys and trains, ferries, and even skateboards, scooters, golf carts, and electric wheelchairs. Using any of these modes of transportation can be harder or easier, and more or less dangerous, depending on the infrastructure of the place.

There is also some value in getting from place to place in the larger environment, by car, train, airplane, or ship. For some, having an easy way to get to the airport or the train station may be particularly important for the sake of business, recreation, or family obligations.

(i) Aesthetics

Places that are attractive or beautiful to people are better than those that are not, all else being equal. There is often sharp disagreement about which places are beautiful, though there may be a broad consensus in favor of mountain ranges and seascapes. People will sometimes go out of their way, when travelling or buying a house, for the sake of a dramatic view. There is likely also to be a consensus that some features of the landscape are just ugly, and perhaps noisy and smelly besides: garbage dumps, oil refineries, airports, many strip malls, derelict buildings, cell phone towers, and the like.

Beyond beauty and ugliness, people often tie their well-being to a more general 'sense of place', which is a matter of how it feels to be in a particular place and pursue projects there. The main streets of small towns – and newer buildings that imitate them – may strike people as quaint or charming, giving a feeling of community and rootedness in tradition. Suburban neighborhoods may be valued for their pastoral tranquility, giving a feeling of retreat and refuge from the hectic life of the city. Some people may respond to what they feel as the vibrancy of urban neighbor-hoods, which gives their projects an urgency and a hipness they find appealing. Of course, there is usually disagreement about the feeling of a place: old rural villages can also strike people as backward and oppressive, their imitations as crass and phony, suburban neighborhoods as sterile and monotonous, and urban neighborhoods as raucous and dangerous.

(j) Security

People also value a sense of security, which is broader and more general than any of the values considered so far. A sense of security is confidence in the stability of the places that support a particular way of living: if a place is healthy and beautiful, it will remain healthy and beautiful; the opportunities of today will still be there tomorrow, with no new obstacles arising along the way.

As with safety, a sense of security may largely be an aesthetic matter, and the perception of stability more important to people than the underlying reality. Whether a given place really is secure is in part a matter of sustainability, discussed below.

(k) Community

Community here is understood in the narrow sense of the network of relationships among people who live within a particular place. A broader sense of community is linked to questions of justice, which I will discuss in the next section.

Humans are social animals. We need other people for more than just the possibility of trade; many of the values already considered, from education to recreation, depend on the help of others. In community, we have the possibility of finding friends and potential partners, and of finding help in pursuing our various projects. This 'social capital' is built up by casual interac-tion among neighbors, and in the more formal settings of neigh-borhood associations, social clubs, civic organizations, religious groups, sports clubs, and so on.[6] We also find various kinds of limits in our relationships with others: in competition and disapproval, the social enforcement of mores, and so on.

There are, of course, disagreements over what community ought to look like and how strong a network ought to be – from the isolated privacy associated with big cities to the intrusive intimacy associated with small towns, and everything in between. Jane Jacobs argued that, in older urban neighborhoods, residents had plenty of opportunity to meet casually on the street, in shops, and in public places, providing some of the glue that holds society together without intruding into private spaces and private lives. New Urbanist architects and planners often cite this as an explicit goal of their efforts to revive older ways of building streetscapes, squares, and parks. In traditional American suburbs, on the other hand, there is much less of a possibility for casual interaction because of the different structure of commercial development and the lack of public spaces. So, suburban residents either remain isolated from one another, seeking their social capital elsewhere, or else invite neighbors into their private spaces and private lives – a form of community Jacobs called 'togetherness'.[7]

4.2. Who gets to benefit from this place, and who does not? (Justice)

The value people place on their own well-being may be thought of in terms of obligations they have to themselves: if flourishing is good, then people owe it to themselves to find or create situations in which they can flourish. Some of the values of the good life might also imply at least indirect obligations to others, especially to children and other family members, as necessary for the good life of the individual.

Matters of justice, by contrast, concern the mutual relations among people and the mutual obligations that bind us together.

The most basic question of justice is: What do we owe to one another? The question can be taken in a narrow sense to refer to the distribution of rewards and punishments, but it can also be taken in a broader sense to refer to mutual respect and mutual concern. In this broader sense, for example, a minimum requirement of justice might be that people ought not to harm one another. How to define 'harm', and how far to go beyond this minimum requirement in creating a just society are matters of dispute.

In the ethics of the built environment, the central question of justice is whether and to what extent we have an obligation to ensure that other people have access to opportunities in their environment to secure good lives for themselves – from clean air and water to home-ownership and mobility to education and employment – and an obligation to share the economic, social, and environmental costs of acting on these opportunities. There is a long history, in the United States and elsewhere, of excluding particular groups from some opportunities while imposing on those same groups a larger share of the costs of keeping those opportunities open for others.

(a) Community

When I discussed community as part of well-being, I used the term in a narrow and self-interested sense. The question was: Will the other people who live in this place help me to flourish? Here, I use the term in a broader and more prescriptive sense. The questions are: Do we have an obligation to help others to flourish, or at least to stay out of their way? What ought we to contribute to the common good? and: How far does this community of obligation extend?

The question of extent is particularly important. It may be that the way one person lives has an adverse impact on people who live on the other side of the world or on the other side of the railroad tracks. It may in some way harm people who are alive now or people who will live a century from now. It may even harm non-human animals, plants, and ecological systems. Do we have an obligation to take such impacts into account and arrange our lives so as to minimize them? If we are part of a community that spans the globe and crosses the boundaries of generations and of species, then we may be subject to a very broad conception of the common good that would seem to give serious moral weight to every little decision we make.

(b) Class

People may find themselves excluded from opportunities in the built environment for economic reasons as well as for social reasons linked to their perceived economic status.

A transportation system based on the personal automobile is closed to anyone who cannot afford to own, insure, maintain, and fuel a car. Those who use public transit for financial reasons may find they cannot afford to live in neighborhoods near convenient transit stops because those neighborhoods are increasingly inhabited by more affluent people who use transit for other reasons. Those who start out at an economic disadvantage may have a hard time becoming mobile enough to take advantage of the economic opportunities available in other parts of their region.

The spatial mismatch between employment and housing is particularly acute for the urban poor, who may live in public housing or in neglected inner-city neighborhoods but work in menial jobs out in the suburbs, where they cannot afford to live and to which they can travel only by bus and on foot.[8] The mismatch also affects those who provide basic services to more affluent communities, who often cannot afford to live in the communities they serve. When public officials speak of the lack of affordable housing in particular areas, they are often referring to housing for teachers, firefighters, police officers, civil servants and early-career professionals rather than for the poor.

In order to function properly, the built environment includes features most people would rather not see, including cell phone towers, power plants, high-tension power lines and substations, sewage treatment plants, airports, and interstate highways. In the jargon of planning, these are LULUs: locally unwanted land uses. When it comes time to decide on the location of such features, local residents often respond with NIMBY: not in my backyard. Residents of more affluent neighborhoods often have the time, the means, and the political clout successfully to fight off LULUs, while residents of less affluent neighborhoods do not. If all else fails, more affluent people are more likely to be able to move away from the problem, putting LULUs out of sight and out of mind. As a consequence, the very people who have the most difficulty taking advantage of opportunities in the built environment may be the ones who bear a disproportionate share of the costs.

(c) Race

Racial and ethnic minorities have also been excluded from opportunities in the built environment. This was most stark in the American South during the Jim Crow era, when African Americans were barred by law from living in the same neighborhoods, going to the same schools, or using the same public accommodations as white Americans. Racial segregation was not limited to the South, however. Until the 1970s, as already noted in the last chapter, redlining was the officially sanctioned practice of the Federal Housing Administration (FHA), which denied mortgage guarantees to any neighborhood containing 'inharmonious racial groups': the presence of just one black family in a white neighborhood was perceived as a threat to the stability of housing values.[9]

Even today, long after the passage of civil rights laws and the institution of fair lending, patterns of segregation still persist throughout the United States. There are suburban enclaves that are predominantly white and suburban enclaves that are predominantly black; many inner-city neighborhoods have for decades been predominantly black, though recent trends towards gentrification in some cities have raised distinctly racial tensions. The whole picture has been complicated by the influx of immigrants from South and Central America and from South and East Asia, all establishing spaces of their own in metropolitan areas.[10]

A further complication comes from the difficulty of determining the extent to which patterns of segregation and unequal opportunity are the result of overt discrimination, and the extent to which they are tied to economic class and other factors. William Julius Wilson has argued that the intensification of inner-city dislocation and the persistence of a black urban underclass after 1970 can more plausibly be explained in terms of a broader 'economic organization', only some of which can in turn be explained in terms of racism, present or past. So, while overt racism in the present may still be a factor in cutting many in minority communities off from opportunities to live a better life, it may no longer be the most important factor. One piece of evidence for this is the fact that the urban underclass began its descent into what Wilson characterizes as social pathology at the same time as a black middle class was growing and strengthening.[11]

(d) Sex/gender

Historically, women and men in the United States have engaged the built environment differently, in large measure because of the different socially defined roles they have played. The first suburbs were often built with the nuclear family in mind, with the mother expected to stay home and care for children while the father commuted into the city for work. Social expectations of men and women may have changed but the patterns of development continue. It is possible those patterns themselves serve to reinforce old expectations, making life easier for families that follow conventional gender roles and more difficult for those that do not. Suburban households may work best when one parent, usually the mother, is available to serve as chauffeur to the children, taking them to and from school, to and from soccer practice.

It may be difficult to make the case that the 'soccer mom' is a symbol of sexual discrimination in the built environment. If there is discrimination involved, someone might argue, it is surely a matter of social expectations rather than suburban development per se; there could just as easily be a 'soccer dad'. This may be so, but then the forms of the built environment may not be doing much to help overcome social expectations either, say by allowing older children to get where they need to go on foot or by other means. Then again, there are some aspects of the environment that clearly are discriminatory, as when public facilities for changing diapers are available only in women's restrooms.

Other possible barriers to women in the built environment concern the perception of safety. There are situations in which women are likely to feel much less safe than men, often because they really are less safe. A woman riding on public transport or walking down a city street alone at night may become the target of sexual harassment or even sexual assault. Knowing this may cause a woman to think twice about going even to some place or event that is important to her, effectively closing off part of her environment.

(e) Marital/family status

Parts of the built environment and some opportunities may be closed off to people because of their family status. Suitable housing and services may not be available for a particular kind of household or, in the case of singles and same-sex partnerships, there may be overt discrimination.

The practice of 'vasectomy zoning' is a bizarre instance of exclusion on the basis of family status. Suburban development has historically been associated with the traditional nuclear family. Providing services for families with children is expensive, however, especially when the school-age population grows quickly. As a general rule, the tax revenue generated by single-family homes is inadequate to cover the cost of such services.

So, some local governments have made it clear that families with children should not move into certain new developments, as public schools and other services would not be expanded to accommodate them. In these instances, at least, households without children have an advantage over nuclear families.

(f) Physical ability

The physical structures of the built environment may presuppose a particular level of physical ability. A multi-story building with no elevator, for example, is accessible only to those who can walk or climb stairs. The pedestrian signals at a busy intersection may provide safety only for those who can see, the curb may accommodate only those who can step down and step up, and – given the dominance of the automobile – the distance to the other side may be safe only for those who can run and who have good timing. The automobile itself makes physical and mental demands upon the driver, demands some people are unable to meet.

The built environment of the United States has recently become more accessible to people with physical disabilities, due largely to the Americans with Disabilities Act (ADA). Curb cuts, ramps, elevators and chair lifts, audible pedestrian signals, paratransit services, and so on, have begun to lower barriers to full participation in economic, cultural, and civic life.

(g) Other species

The environments of human beings overlap with the environments of other species. They provide opportunities for and impose constraints on us, and we do the same for them. When we humans set out to alter an environment to suit ourselves, a large part of what we are doing is favoring some species over others. In the suburbs, certain varieties of grasses, flowering plants, shrubs, and trees are lavished with food and water, while many other species of plant are ruthlessly eradicated. As the alterations take hold, some species are able to adapt and even thrive in the new environment while some, who can survive only in very particular habitats, do not. Robins, English sparrows, starlings, squirrels, chipmunks, house mice, Norway rats, cockroaches, crabgrass, and dandelions do well in cities and suburbs, as do various microscopic organisms that find humans and their buildings to be genial hosts. At the other extreme, species may be threatened or even driven to extinction by urban development.

At times, humans and other animals come into direct conflict, annoying and threatening one another. Some threats to people are pervasive but hard to perceive directly, as with mosquitoes that carry West Nile virus or deer ticks that carry Lyme disease. Other threats are more visible, like a rattlesnake sunning itself on the front step of a suburban house. As metropolitan areas grow further out into surrounding lands, the potential for direct human–animal conflict grows with it. In extreme cases, people can become prey for large animals in their own neighborhoods, as with mountain lions in Colorado or alligators in Florida.

For most people, it may simply be obvious that human interests should always predominate. Ours is the right and the ability to change our environment to suit ourselves, they might declare. Leaving aside for the moment issues of ecological sustainability, it is at least worth asking the question of whether we might owe some consideration to other species for their own sake, not just for ours.[12] Most people are at least open to the idea that dogs and cats deserve some respect and even, in the case of a recent rise in the number of public parks intended for dogs and their owners, direct provision of public services. Whether respect should also be extended to wild animals and plants is at least open to debate.

(h) Other generations

Age has already been introduced as an issue in the built environment, especially as regards the well-being of the old and the young and their ability to gain access to what they need from

the environment. The concern of justice towards other generations is both more general and more broad. For one thing, gen-
erational concerns are not necessarily tied to kinship: they are
not just about what parents owe their children, for example, but
what everyone in an older generation may owe to everyone in a
younger generation. More than this, the intergenerational obligations may go in any direction: those of the middle generations
may have obligations toward their elders and other obligations
toward the younger generation; the oldest generation may have
still other obligations toward all of the younger generations, and
the youngest generations toward all of their elders.

More controversial are the obligations those who are living
might have to those who are not yet living, and perhaps even to
those who are no longer living. The relationships among living
generations are asymmetrical, and the resulting obligations are
to some degree non-reciprocal: the obligations of parents toward
their children are very different from the obligations of children
toward their parents, and children cannot reasonably be expected
to fully repay their parents for all of the care they receive.[13] With
future generations, there can be no possibility of reciprocity:
whatever we may owe them, they will never be able to give us
anything but praise or blame for the choices we have made that
affect them, just as we may praise or blame our ancestors for
making the world into which we were born.

The question remains: What, if anything, do we owe to future
generations? We will not be able to leave them a world exactly
like the one into which we were born, with precisely the same
opportunities, constraints, and risks. We will not be able to leave
them reserves of oil equal to what we have now, for example, or
landscapes precisely as we have known. History does not work
that way. We may be able to leave them some knowledge, some
scope for creativity and critical thought, some economic opportunity, some technological options, and so on. We may also try
not to leave them with the economic, social, and environmental
costs of our current ways of living, whether in the form of budget

deficits, entrenched inequality, pollution and waste, or a radically altered climate.

In short, we may try to leave future generations a world that is better in some ways than the one we have known – more opportunities, fewer risks – or at least a world that is not significantly worse by our own lights. There is a further problem, though. We may try to leave to the future a world that is better or worse by our own lights, but culture and values themselves may change so future generations may judge our legacy by very different standards. What we may owe them, in that case, is to leave a built environment that is open and flexible enough to support other visions of a good life.[14]

4.3. How long can this place last? (Sustainability)

Nothing lasts forever. However good our intentions may be, however thoughtful we may be in making our way in the world, we are still bound by the basic rule that things fall apart, and that the energy required to hold things together or to put them back together will not always be available. Somewhere, off in the future, lies the end of civilization; somewhere beyond that is the extinction of *Homo sapiens*, and far beyond that the destruction of the Earth, very likely a few billion years from now when the Sun becomes a red giant and engulfs the three innermost planets of the solar system. The ultimate fate of the universe itself is a matter of speculation. Whatever ethical or practical concerns we may have about sustainability, they work at a much narrower time-scale, bound up together with the obligations we may have to the next few generations.

Another way of coming at this is to see that all human projects will be defeated in the end, but some projects may be self-defeating while others may be more likely to perpetuate themselves for a while and perhaps even adapt to changes in the

broader context. A project defeats itself when some of its consequences serve to undermine the conditions that make the project
possible in the first place. Each of the various projects that shape
the built environment can be examined in these terms, from
the pursuit of the perfect lawn to the ongoing expansion of a
transportation system based on the private automobile.

(a) Economic sustainability

Individuals, households, and governments at various levels all
need money, or at least something to exchange, in order to carry
out their various projects. Some projects require long-term commitments that can tie up economic resources, narrowing the
scope for pursuing other projects. If such a project expands, it
may eventually call for more resources than are actually available.
Then, either the project must stop or change course, or, if the
project in its current form has become indispensable, bankruptcy
looms. Owners of old houses might recognize a project of this
sort as a 'money pit'.

The rapid growth of metropolitan areas in the United States could
be seen as creating a whole series of money pits. Governments at
various levels spend money to build new infrastructure – roads,
sewers, and so on – at the expanding edge of development while
older infrastructure continues to need maintenance and repair.
While growth and development may generate new tax revenue
in the short term, growth will eventually move on to other areas.
When the local building boom ends, a municipality may find
itself committed to the increasing costs of maintaining a widely
dispersed infrastructure of streets, low-density neighborhoods,
and industrial parks even as tax revenue levels off and starts to
decline. Even before the onset of the financial crisis in 2008, many
inner-ring suburbs were already coping with problems of decay
and abandonment usually associated with inner cities.[15]

The financial crisis might be seen as exposing the economic
unsustainability of at least some kinds of metropolitan growth.

For a time, it seemed as though the economy could keep growing as long as housing values kept rising, and that housing values could keep rising as long as the economy kept growing. As it turned out, keeping this cycle going required lenders and borrowers to take greater and greater risks, and those risks were divided up and distributed throughout the financial system. In hindsight, it seems inevitable that the whole scheme would fall apart, with terrible consequences.

This is, of course, a gross oversimplification of the crisis. Still, I think there is just enough truth in it to give us pause: before we commit ourselves to personal choices and public policies aimed at rebuilding the housing bubble, we should consider whether there might be some other, more secure economic foundation for civilized life as we know it, or perhaps some other, more economically sustainable way of organizing civilized life in the landscape.

(b) Cultural sustainability

The choice of where and how to live is complex, informed by a host of cultural images and ideals. In some cases, however, it seems that the very act of reaching for an ideal pushes it further out of reach. In the built environment, the landscape itself serves as a kind of cultural resource, one that can be transformed, its value undermined, as soon as it is appropriated for cultural ends. The paradigm case is the family that moves to the suburbs to get away from the city, drawn by the image of a tranquil, pastoral landscape, only to find that the landscape becomes less tranquil and less pastoral with each passing year.[16] More residents arrive, followed by commerce and industry, and with them come traffic congestion, noise, and light pollution. The hapless family may try to move away from all this, out to a new home at the new edge of development, but soon enough they will find themselves boxed in again.

The problem may lie with the pastoral ideal itself: almost by definition, not everyone can live in the middle landscape,

balanced as it is supposed to be between the city and the wilderness. If everyone tries to live there at once, it simply becomes the
city – even if it is a peculiar sort of city that still pretends to be
something other than what it is.[17]

(c) Ecological sustainability

All human projects are intertwined with and supported by systems
of physical, chemical and biological relationships that make up
the natural world. Human projects bring about changes in those
relationships. That is the whole point of human projects: we reor-
ganize parts of the world to suit ourselves and to secure what we
value. The problem is that the workings of the world are complex,
and bringing about a change that suits us will usually also bring
about other changes that do not suit us so well. An ecological
system that supports our projects today may, under the accu-
mulation of unintended consequences, shift to a new state that
will no longer support our projects tomorrow and the projects
of future generations. This, in simplest terms, is the problem of
ecological sustainability.[18]

Historically, the problem of sustainability has been local: a city
here or a kingdom over there has either overshot or undermined
its own ecological basis. Easter Island is often held up as an
object lesson in unsustainable practice, as the inhabitants used
up resources that could be replenished only very slowly, especially the slow-growing palm trees native to the island. In the
world at large, as human numbers and the scope of our activities
have expanded, and as our technological powers have increased,
we now face the prospect that we are undermining the props
of civilization at the global as well as at the regional and local
levels.

Much that we take for granted about the Earth is changing around us, from the diversity and abundance of life to the
availability of arable land and potable water to the stability and
predictability of the climate. This may not yet spell the doom of

our species or of civilization, but it is very likely to make life in our various places more precarious and more difficult.

Most Americans have committed themselves to a way of life that requires the consumption of large amounts of energy, much of it from fossil fuels, to heat and cool our homes, to power our many appliances, and to keep our cars moving from home to work, from work to the store, and so on. This puts us up against two different problems of sustainability.

The first is that fossil fuels are not a renewable resource. There is debate as to whether world oil production has already passed its peak, but it is clear enough that, sooner or later, it will become more difficult and more expensive to extract oil from the ground, refine it, and get the products to market. Natural gas and coal face a similar prospect. It is not yet clear whether or how we can go on living in our current built environment when we can no longer count on cheap, plentiful reserves of fossil fuels.

The second problem of sustainability is that burning fossil fuels releases into the atmosphere carbon that was sequestered by plants and animals millions of years ago, contributing to global climate change. As the climate changes, it becomes harder to predict local conditions and the behavior of local ecological systems, which in turn makes it harder to plan human projects. Because of a shift in the jet stream, for example, there may or may not be enough rain for crops next year or enough water in the reservoir to support the human population of the region.

It seems as though questions of ecological sustainability should loom large in any discussion of the future of the built environment. One question, of course, is whether current ways of building and living in the United States are sustainable given our expectations and the technology available to us. The really interesting question, though, is whether and how to build different kinds of places that make it possible for us to live both richly – in terms of the various values already discussed here – and sustainably.

4.4. Who should make decisions about this place? (Legitimacy)

In the best sense of the term, politics can be thought of as the extension of ethics into the public realm. Ethics is mainly about decisions made by individuals based on their own understanding of what is good and what is right. Politics, in the best sense, is mainly about how people should work out the arrangements whereby they can live together, especially the processes and institutions through which decisions affecting whole communities are made and enforced. At their best, political institutions and the decisions that issue from them can also be informed by an understanding of what is good and what is right.

A central political question in the built environment is whether and to what degree government, at whatever level, has a legitimate role to play in constraining and directing individual choices in the service of well-being, justice and sustainability. Free-market advocates argue that most decisions about housing, transportation, and so on should be made by individuals acting on their own in the marketplace, leaving to government only the task of establishing and enforcing the ground rules of market interactions. As it happens, however, governments at all levels have played a much more significant role in shaping the landscape, making some ways of building and ways of living easier than others, supporting some forms of transportation while neglecting others, and enforcing the strict separation of uses that now defines American metropolitan areas.

(a) Property

The whole idea of private property is that, all else being equal, only the owner of a given piece of property can legitimately make decisions about it: whether and how it should be preserved, altered, used, or discarded. This applies to parcels of land as well as to smaller and more portable pieces of property, and it applies to property owned by corporations as well as to property owned by individuals. When much of the landscape is held as private property then, all else being equal, decisions that shape the resulting landscape are distributed among the various owners, each of whom may have a different vision of what makes a good place.

The protection of property rights is one of the cornerstones of the American political system, but property rights have not usually been regarded as absolute.[19] Zoning regulations, for example, were first put in place in order to prevent noxious uses of land near places where people live. Those regulations have developed into what is called a 'Euclidean' zoning system characterized by a strict separation of uses: residential development here, commercial development over there, and industrial development somewhere else, preferably out of sight.

If I wanted to build a tallow-rendering works (an example from the past) or a convenience store (an example from the present) on my property in a residential neighborhood, the city would step in to prevent me from doing so. Further regulations apply within zones, governing everything from the distance between buildings and the street ('setback'), the size and proportions of buildings, the height and size of signs, to the percentage of the land covered by impermeable surface, the number of trees, and so on. In commercial zones, some kinds of commerce may be forbidden altogether, as when bars, shops selling pornography, or even fast-food restaurants are barred from operating within a certain distance of a school.

Through zoning and other regulations, the rights of landowners to do what they want with their land is, to some degree at least, subordinated to the public interest. The important ethical questions, then, are how far property rights extend, and how compelling a public interest must be in order to justify curtailing property rights.

(b) Citizen involvement

The idea that rights may be limited in the face of compelling public interest raises some further questions, of course: What is the public interest? and: Who gets to say what it is? One core idea of democratic forms of government is that, in order to be legitimate, decisions about the public interest should be made by citizens themselves, whether directly through public meetings and referenda, or indirectly through the election of public officials.

There are often opportunities for direct citizen involvement in decisions affecting land use. The public may be invited to participate in a planning process, for example, or to attend a hearing about a zoning variance. Controversial decisions, such as a proposal to allow a particular big-box retail store to be built in a particular area, can bring local citizens out in large numbers, along with activists from various camps, all fighting hard to push the decision one way or another.

There is always a question of how seriously the public is taken in such processes. Public hearings can often be more like public showings: the decision has all but been made by officials working behind closed doors; the decision is presented to the public, which is then allowed to show its support or vent its rage before the decision is implemented. Along the way, there may be various efforts to co-opt opposition groups, manipulate the process, exclude certain people or certain groups, and to cut short the debate. In other cases, though, public reaction and discussion may be allowed to shape the decision, to one degree or another, even to the point that citizens are directly involved in the earliest stages of the process. At this end of the scale, when things work unusually well, a public consensus may emerge early on that shapes the final outcome.[20]

The question, then, is whether and how citizens should be directly involved in public decisions that affect land use and, if they are involved, how to take their contributions seriously. Issues of justice arise here as well, in the question of what measures should be taken to ensure that everyone who should have access to the decision-making process in fact has such access. Providing transportation and childcare to make it easier for people to attend public meetings, for example, may turn out to be an important part of ensuring the legitimacy of the process.

(c) Leadership

Direct citizen involvement is not always possible or practical, given the scope and the number of decisions to be made. Even in those cases when citizen participation seems like a really good idea, the debate may degenerate into entrenched verbal warfare between competing groups. Anyone who has attended public meetings knows there are always some obstructionists, not just NIMBYs but also those who are sometimes called CAVE people: Citizens Against Virtually Everything.

At some point, public officials may simply have to cut through all of this disagreement and make a decision, risking public disapproval and putting re-election or reappointment on the line. This is the dilemma of leadership in a democratic political system: elected officials are supposed to represent the people, but in doing so they are often torn between doing what they know is popular and doing what they think is really in the public interest. The trick is to know when the time has come to cut off an unproductive debate and make a decision that will anger or disappoint a significant number of people.

(d) Transparency

Since there are a number of decisions that perhaps should be left to elected and appointed officials, the question remains as to the extent to which their decision-making process should be open to public scrutiny. Officials in a democratic political system are supposed to derive their authority from the consent of the people, from which it follows that they should be accountable to the people for their actions. Citizens cannot hold officials accountable if they do not know what those officials are up to, which suggests that government decision-making processes should be transparent.

Public officials occasionally argue that there is a compelling public interest in secrecy, although this most typically arises when national security is at stake. Nevertheless, the argument is some-times made that some decisions about land use are best made behind closed doors, as when there is a delicate negotiation over tax breaks and other incentives for a corporation to build a factory that will provide economic opportunity for local residents. Again, this may be part of the balancing act of leadership in a democratic political system, especially since, in the long run, citizens may find ways of holding officials accountable even for their decisions about transparency and secrecy.

(e) Coordination

In the United States, one of the most pressing issues of legiti-macy is the fragmentation of political authority. There is a long American tradition of home rule, the idea that public decisions about land use should be made as close to home as possible, typi-cally at the city or county level. In practice, this means dozens of local jurisdictions may be competing for economic development and tax revenue in the same region, and many of those jurisdic-tions either do not plan for growth or do so in ways that may be self-defeating. State governments and the federal government also have jurisdiction over some elements of the built environ-ment, particularly transportation infrastructure, but may not be responsive to the interests of regions and municipalities. Any international agreements – on climate change, for example, or free trade – would also have consequences that would ramify through the built environment down to the local level.

Adding to the complexity, many Americans have in effect subjected themselves to the authority of private governments in the act of buying a home: home-owners associations and con-dominium associations often take on some of the functions of government at the neighborhood level, though often without the accountability of public government. To be subject to a private government is to take on many responsibilities while giving up many rights, such as the right to change the color of a house or to plant a particular kind of shrub.

To the extent all of these different levels of government pull against one another, each asserting its own rights and preroga-tives, there is less likely to be an effective response to problems in the built environment. Perhaps most important, there is often a mismatch between the scale of problems and the scale of the government authority with the power to address them. So those with the most authority over land use work at the municipal and county level, but their decisions have consequences that create problems at the regional level. State and federal officials cannot do much to address the roots of these problems, since they are rightly concerned with larger-scale problems and, in any case, usually lack the authority to intervene in local land-use decisions. The most they can do is establish a more general legal framework for the state or the nation within which local officials might make better decisions.

One response to this situation has been to develop a new political authority that is matched more precisely to problems that arise at the regional level. Regional planning bodies of one sort or another have sprung up around the country, though they are usually beset by controversies over their legitimacy and their effectiveness. Even if a regional planning body can overcome the clash of local interests and arrive at a good plan or good rules for the region, it may nevertheless lack the will or the authority to implement the plan or enforce rules at the local level. Many regional planning authorities have been left toothless by local governments that are jealous of their jurisdiction over the built environment.

5.   Using the Framework

The framework just presented has yet to prove its worth. It will do this to the extent it helps people make better decisions about projects that shape our common environment. But what, ethically speaking, is a better decision? What does a good decision look like?

Throughout the book, I have been sketching the outlines of an experiential approach to ethical decision making. The core idea of the approach is that choosing and pursuing projects is always to some degree a matter of trial and error. Our decisions should be based on our best understanding of the place in which the project is to be carried out and our clearest accounting of what we value and what we hope for. When we choose a project together, our process of choosing should be as fair and open as we can make it. When we carry out the project, we should be attentive to all the big and little ways it does and does not meet our expectations, and we should revise our understanding of the place, our project, our values, and ourselves accordingly. We should then carry that new understanding with us into the process of revising the project, and into other decisions about other projects. On this account, ethical inquiry and decision making are open-ended: our decisions may get better and better, but they will never be as good as they can be.

Now, it might seem as though engaging in this sort of deliberation for every decision about every project in the built environment is a tall order, and that the complexity of the framework only makes it taller. Imagine trying to answer all of these questions before making any little decision, even stepping off the front porch on the way to work: Is this good for me? Does this serve the cause of justice? Is this a sustainable practice? Do I have the right to make this decision? By the time I have asked all of the subordinate questions, about health, safety, community, race, class, future generations, and so on, I could well find myself paralyzed, my foot poised eternally above the pavement, unable to take a single step while the deliberation goes on.

We do not usually live this way. Most of the time, we live and act automatically on the basis of decisions already made – consciously or not, by ourselves or by others – at some point in the past. We are creatures of habit, especially when our environment is relatively stable. When something does change in our environment, or is about to change, we make snap judgments about the change in light of our established habits. How well we do in the long run, living automatically in this way, depends on the quality of past decisions and on how well our habits are attuned to different circumstances.

There are occasions, though, when it might be best to stop ourselves, to examine our own habits and snap judgments, and to consider revising them in light of a clearer understanding of our circumstances. It is on such occasions, I think, that the framework I have presented may be useful.

The snap judgments we make are often ethical judgments, whether we recognize them as such or not. Sprawl? Bad! Density? Bad! Apartment buildings? Bad! Diversity? Good! Rising home values? Very good! If we were to stop and examine any one of these, we might discover that the underlying values are actually very complex. Someone who judges sprawl to be bad, for instance, may be reacting to a number of different and very particular features of a place and may ultimately have to admit that other particular features of that same place are really not so bad.

One occasion for examining snap judgments more carefully arises when there are tensions and contradictions between two judgments. For example, how can it be that someone who lives within the fabric of a metropolitan area views both sprawl and density as bad? Sprawl is often identified as a specific pattern of low-density development, and higher density patterns are sometimes touted as an antidote to sprawl. Yet, even though the two are taken to be opposites, people often hate both of them – an apparent contradiction that has puzzled planners and anti-sprawl advocates for years. How can the tension be resolved? In practical terms, it does not generally work to flee to the countryside to escape both sprawl and density, because such flight is part of the process that generates sprawl in the first place. It may be there is something else going on here, some strange confluence of assumptions, attitudes, and judgments that needs to be sorted out by a more careful analysis.

Or, again, there is often a tension between a snap judgment in favor of diversity and a snap judgment in favor of rising home values, at least in conditions where the market tends to favor homogeneous neighborhoods. There is a widespread perception in the United States that the best way to ensure stability in the value of a house is for it to be surrounded by houses worth more or less the same amount of money and occupied by people in more or less the same walks of life. So, while diversity in general may be judged to be good, social and economic diversity in this particular neighborhood may be judged to be bad. So, then, where will diversity really be welcomed, and how much of it? This, too, seems to call out for careful investigation.

Another occasion for examining snap judgments arises when there is an important decision to be made about a common project but the parties to the decision disagree. Suppose someone for whom sprawl and density are both bad has to work with someone for whom sprawl is bad but density is good, and suppose the project they are working on would increase the density of development in a given area. Either they must find a way to work through their differences by appealing to more basic values, or they must go their separate ways. Otherwise promising projects have been abandoned over such disagreements, and it is because of such disagreements that the politics of metropolitan growth can sometimes get ugly.

Then again, the politics of metropolitan growth can also make strange bedfellows, which is a further occasion for examining snap judgments. How can it be that people who disagree with one another in many other domains of private and public life sometimes come together and make common cause over metropolitan growth?[1] Sometimes they want to achieve the same ends but disagree over the means. Sometimes they agree on the means, such as political power for the movement as a whole, in order to push their own particular ends.

So it is that big-tent ideas like 'smart growth' can draw the support of environmental groups, industry groups, government agencies, and planning professionals, each with its own agenda. Such a coalition can hold together so long as the ideas are pitched at a sufficiently high level of generality and in the face of a perceived common problem. Once the coalition starts to get down to the details, or once it starts to have some success, the rifts within the movement will start to open. Here, again, some fine-grained analysis can help people to clarify, for themselves and for others, what they are really after and on what basis they might be able to work together.

Drawing this together, I would suggest there are at least four uses of the framework in ethical deliberation (Table 5.1). First, the framework can serve as a tool for analyzing the complex values and assumptions that underlie what seem to be simple ethical judgments. By drawing finer distinctions, we may be able

Table 5.1

Four Ways to Use the Framework
Reveal hidden complexity in ethical judgments.
Identify points of agreement and disagreement.
Focus discussion and deliberation.
Search for new possibilities.

to expose tensions as well as forge new connections among our values. I have already begun to illustrate how this might work.

I have also started to illustrate how people trying to decide on a common project could use the framework in a second way, to see more clearly where they agree and where they disagree. If you find out I disapprove of sprawl while you claim to favor sprawl, that actually tells you very little about the depths of our disagreement or the grounds we might have for agreement. You and I might actually agree in our views on economic justice, for example, while we disagree over the relative value of mobility. Once we have used the framework to bring this to light, it is still up to us to figure out whether and how we are going to get along and work on projects together, but at least we have a better sense of our starting point.

Should we decide to talk through our differences, the framework can then come into play in a third way, focusing our discussion where it is most likely to do some good. If you and I happen to agree in making particular assumptions about economic justice, for example, we may be able to set that issue aside and focus instead on a point on which we clearly disagree or about which we are both uncertain. In this way, for all its complexity, the framework may help us to simplify our deliberations.

Finally, the framework may be used as a spur to creativity, pointing out new directions in which projects might go. If deliberation stays at the level of habits and snap judgments, the options we can see may be very limited: sprawl or density, cars or transit. It might be that none of the options on the table are very promising or even very palatable. By turning the discussion instead towards a fine-grained exploration of more basic values, such as mobility or economic justice, it might occur to us that there are other, unforeseen options that allow us to fulfill more of these values at the same time. If a local transit authority is fixated on the either-or choice between buses and trains, for example, it may never occur to them there are other options in between. Looking instead at the underlying values, balancing mobility and security with economic sustainability, and so on, it becomes easier to imagine some of these other options: bus rapid transit, for example, or intermodal transportation hubs.

I should emphasize once again that the framework plays a relatively modest role in deliberation. It is not intended as an algorithm for solving problems, nor is it a scorecard for assigning value to particular places. Rather, the framework is intended as an analytic tool that can support an experiential approach to ethical decision making, helping people to identify and tease apart the many questions they might need to address. It serves as a reminder of the many different values that may be at stake in a decision, values about which we may or may not agree.

5.1. Reveal hidden complexity in ethical judgments

When we make snap judgments about a change in our environment, we often couch them in terms that are comfortably vague. Everyone knows, or thinks they know, what sprawl is, and most people disapprove of it just as they disapprove of injustice or dishonesty. Who could possibly be in favor of such things? In the same way, everyone approves of a higher quality of life, more security, more freedom, and more of particular things like green space. Again, who could possibly be opposed to such things?

As already noted, it is easy to agree about the value or disvalue of these things so long as the terms remain comfortably vague, that is, general enough to gloss over real disagreements in practice. No one approves of injustice, but we may disagree sharply about whether a particular project or policy is unjust. Everyone approves of a high quality of life, but only because the term 'quality' has almost no actual content: we can fill it with anything we choose. For one, quality of life is entirely a function of economic prosperity while, for another, quality of life is pegged to values and relationships that may actually be harmed by too much prosperity.[2]

The hidden ethical complexity of snap judgments may be most obvious when a vague term marks a cultural rift rather than a broad consensus. Everyone hates sprawl and loves green space, but opinion is split on density. For many, as already noted, density is a code word for all of the evils of urbanization, evoking the filth, corruption, and danger of early industrial cities. Density is also loaded with the baggage of discrimination by race and class: high-density developments are where *they* live, you know, *them* (whoever they are). For at least a few people, though, density is a code word for all that is good about old urbanism, the setting for a rich and vibrant civic and cultural life in public spaces, a precondition for real democracy, the antidote to sprawl, and the key to sustainability.

Notice what has happened here: when I push on the disagreement over a comfortably vague term, it resolves itself into much more specific judgments about which there is likely to be still sharper disagreement. The analysis could go a step further, as even these more specific judgments employ vague terms. Density is the antidote to sprawl? Well, what *is* sprawl, exactly, and why do we need an antidote to it? Judgments about sprawl break down further into more specific judgments about well-being, justice, and sustainability, which can break down further into judgments about health, economic equity, and so on.

This kind of analysis can have uncomfortable consequences. Suddenly, people who were content to think of themselves as allies fighting against sprawl or for a higher quality of life may be forced to recognize that they actually have very different goals, and even that they do not really understand one another. Suddenly, it may become clear that many of the more specific judgments revealed by analysis may not hold up very well under scrutiny. A snap judgment may be rooted in unwarranted assumptions about the way the world works: a selective reading of history, for example, or a misinterpretation of scientific theory. It may also be rooted in specific ethical judgments that are suspect, or at least ill-considered, such as discrimination on the basis of race or class.

That the consequences of analysis are uncomfortable is no reason to avoid doing analysis. As with medical treatment, a little discomfort now may help us to avoid more serious pain later on. Hidden disagreements among allies will come to light eventually, when the time comes for them to decide on the practical details of a particular project. Coming to understand their differences beforehand, on the basis of analysis, can help them to figure out what to do about their disagreement. Faulty assumptions and suspect judgments will also come to light, sometimes in costly mistakes or grave ethical offences. Anything we can do to foresee and avoid such outcomes will be worthwhile, even if it does mean that we have to deal with some discomfort right now.

To show what it might look like to analyze a snap judgment, consider the example of green space. It would be difficult to find someone who is opposed to green space in general, but it is easy to find disagreements over particular plans for particular parcels of land. Part of this hinges on the vagueness of the term itself. What kind of space should it be? Does it have to be large, or can it be small? Does there have to be some sort of public access to it, or does private green space count? What qualifies a given space as 'green'? If 'green' is the same as 'natural', then how natural is natural enough? How artificial is too artificial? These are questions of real importance for practice and for policy, especially when there are laws or ordinances mandating a certain amount of green space in and around the built environment. Can we count the planted median of a highway? How about a tennis court in the middle of a condominium development? What about an area of pristine wilderness to which most people are denied access?

The analysis in Table 5.2 is partial in that it is skewed towards green space that is created and maintained at public expense and that is open to public use without discrimination. There is actually likely to be further disagreement about this. People may insist that at least some private land uses should also be considered

Table 5.2

ANALYZING A SNAP JUDGMENT
'Green space is good!'

WELL-BEING

Green space . . .

. . . improves physical and mental health.

. . . increases market value of surrounding properties.

. . . provides an outdoor classroom for environmental education.

. . . can preserve part of the cultural heritage of the community.

. . . provides an appropriate setting for family life.

. . . provides opportunities for relaxation and physical exercise.

. . . is pretty, or at least pleasant.

. . . serves as a refuge from development and noise.

. . . serves as public space for the community.

JUSTICE

Green space . . .

. . . should be created and maintained at community expense.

. . . should make its benefits available to all.

. . . protects habitat for other species.

. . . leaves options open for future generations.

SUSTAINABILITY

Green space . . .

. . . is a good bargain for ongoing public investment.

. . . helps to ensure the continuation of cultural ideals about landscapes.

. . . protects systems that provide vital ecosystem services.

. . . cannot be easily restored once it is lost.

LEGITIMACY

Green space . . .

. . . is best left in public hands.

green space, such as suburban backyards or private country clubs. In those and other cases, some of the value of the green space rests in the fact that access is restricted to people who meet a particular qualification, whether ownership or membership. If nothing else, private green space might be seen as a refuge from the stress and occasional ugliness of over-used public green space. There is likely to be further disagreement about whether green space is best treated as a public good, with decisions left in the hands of public officials, or whether it is best treated as a private commodity.

Even setting these questions aside, the analysis as it stands reveals many opportunities for disagreement in particular situations. For example, the question of whether a patch of woodland should be cleared to make room for a soccer field could open a rift between someone who values green space primarily because it is pretty and because it provides habitat for other species and someone who values green space primarily for its recreational uses. Or, in another situation, the question of whether to charge user-fees for a public park could divide people along a number of different lines. The value of free access to the park as a public good would have to be weighed against the fiscal viability of the park, the quality of the experience of using the park, the effects of overuse on the long-term sustainability of the park, and so on.

There is even room for disagreement about the meaning of more specific terms used in the analysis. Green space may be good in part because it provides opportunities for recreation, but what kinds of recreation should this include? Is it enough for a park to provide a pleasant setting and unpaved walking trails, or should there also be paved trails, different kinds of sports fields, tennis courts, skate parks, and areas just for dogs as well? Not all of these are compatible, especially if space and budgets are limited. That some people are looking for opportunities to hunt or to pursue motorized sports only complicates matters further.

It is worth noting that what goes for 'green space' goes also for 'environmental issues' more broadly. A traditional, middle-of-the road conception of what it means to be an environmentalist in the United States includes some combination of concerns for health, aesthetics, recreation, justice towards other people and future generations, justice towards other species and perhaps ecosystems, and ecological sustainability. Those who think of themselves as environmentalists differ among themselves on the meaning of these concerns, the priority they give to one or another of them, and whether they see their concerns as opposed to or complementary with the concerns of economic prosperity and private property.

5.2. Identify points of agreement and disagreement

In public discussions of metropolitan growth, particular projects can become flashpoints for controversy. Public officials propose to build a new highway or to widen an existing highway. A site is needed for a landfill, a factory, or a big-box retail store. A developer proposes to build an apartment complex in or next to a neighborhood of single-family homes. In these and many other instances, people quickly line up on one side or another, for or against the proposal. Neighbor is pitted against neighbor, citizens against public officials, the public against powerful private interests. It is in these circumstances that surprising alliances and even surprising enmity have their roots. The dispute can play itself out in angry rants at public hearings, slogans on bumper stickers and yard signs, demonstrations, and lawsuits.

I have come to think of such controversies as proxy battles. The conflict is ostensibly about the highway, the landfill, or the apartment building, but these serve as stand-ins for a wide range of value judgments and value conflicts. For the sake of more productive – and maybe less angry – public deliberation, we might do well to step back from the obvious conflict to see more precisely what is at stake. Not only might there be important points of agreement among those who stand opposed to one another but, as in the case of green space, there may be important points of disagreement among allies.

The distinction between the proxy battle and the underlying values runs parallel to a distinction in the literature of negotiation and conflict resolution: positions versus interests.[3] I may take the position that the apartment building should be built next to the neighborhood of single-family homes, and you take the contrary position. If we stick just to our positions, our discussion can quickly degenerate to the point that all we can do is shout our positions at one another, hoping others will rally to our cause and bring some political and legal weaponry with them. If, on the other hand, we discuss our underlying interests, we may find we have some basis for working through our differences towards a resolution that will be at least partially satisfying to both of us. The resolution need not be a mere compromise but, to use the jargon of negotiation, a 'win-win' solution.

Say I favor the apartment building because I think it is important to have inexpensive housing options for people who provide essential services to our community, such as firefighters and teachers. At the same time, I think the apartments could add human diversity and architectural variety to the neighborhood. Besides, I think that, in the long run, Americans should start to build and live at higher densities in order to reduce our demand for energy and to make walking and transit more viable as alternatives to the automobile.

For your part, you worry that most of the new apartment complexes you have seen are ugly, and that the scale of this particular complex will change the character of the community. Suppose, in all fairness, the actual design for this particular complex is widely agreed to be unappealing. You are also concerned renters will be less likely to take care of their property and the neighborhood than owners would be. Besides, you know the real estate market tends to favor homogeneity in a neighborhood, and you do not want to see property values decline. Then, of course, there is the problem of increasing traffic, worries about the safety of the neighborhood, and so on.

Resolving all of our differences, or even just acknowledging them, will be no easy task. Once we consider the more complex assumptions and value judgments that underlie our positions, though, we may be able to see some common ground. You and I both care about the aesthetics of the neighborhood: we want it to be attractive and to have a strong sense of place. I may favor variety while you favor consistency of character, but at least we can share a good laugh over the ugliness of the current design. Designs can be changed, though, if the developer is brought into the conversation. Maybe there is a way to build the apartments to fit in with the architectural character of the community without simply repeating its pattern, a design we could both agree on.

An agreement on aesthetics might not get us very far, but other points of apparent disagreement may be resolved in much the same way. For example, there is no necessary conflict between my interest in affordable housing and your interest in having neighbors who are as invested in the neighborhood as we are. Some units in the complex could be sold as inexpensive condominium units, while others are available for rent. Perhaps units that are rented could be subject to a lease that imposes some restrictions on the activity of the renter regarding the appearance and maintenance of the property.

I should be careful not to overstate the potential for agreement. When it comes right down to it, my approval of the apartment complex may be rooted in snobbish urbanism, and your opposition is rooted in a cultural memory of the tenement slums of industrial cities and in fears about race and class. All our careful negotiations can run aground on deeper cultural rifts – unless, perhaps, we can openly acknowledge our own fundamental biases and perhaps even laugh at them as well. Whether and how we go on from there depends in part on the value each of us places on civility and reasonableness in public discourse.

Another complication in this story is that the developers of the proposed apartment complex have interests of their own that need to be taken into account. Their main interest is in making a profit from land they have bought or would like to buy. In order to do this, they may need to have the land re-zoned for a different residential use, which means at least some of the battle will play itself out in hearings of the local zoning board. Given the costs of construction, market conditions, and any number of regulations regarding the quality of the buildings and their environmental impact, there are limits to their flexibility in responding to public concerns. In the end, if they are to build anything, it will have to include a particular number of units for sale or rent at particular price points. Too much change in one direction or another, and it will no longer be worth their while to build anything. This is not necessarily a good outcome, whatever your position might have been.

Table 5.3 provides a more thorough analysis of a proxy battle concerning an apartment complex. This follows the same pattern as the analysis of green space in the previous section, except that in this case there are two conflicting snap judgments (a.k.a. 'positions') rather than just one. As in the case of green space, there is room for both agreement and disagreement among the value judgments (a.k.a. 'interests') of those who agree in their snap judgments about the project. While the disagreements are much more obvious among the values of those who make opposing snap judgments, there are at least points on which the disagreement is not really very direct. As I have already shown, indirect disagreements leave open at least a little space for a more substantive agreement.

5.3. Focus deliberation

The point of analyzing snap judgments and proxy battles is to turn discussion and deliberation in more productive directions. While each of us may have the privilege of holding and defending our various positions, doing so will not get us very far in working out common projects for us to pursue or even in clearing the way for our private projects. We can get farther by examining the more basic values at stake for each of us, taking advantage of the openings left by the surprising agreements and indirect disagreements we find in the process of analysis.

Table 5.3

ANALYZING A PROXY BATTLE

Responses to a proposal to build an apartment complex next to a neighborhood of single-family homes.

WELL-BEING

An apartment complex . . .

. . . can be architecturally interesting.

. . . provides affordable housing.

. . . contributes to walkability and viability of transit.

. . . increases the vitality of the neighborhood.

. . . increases the diversity of the community.

An apartment complex . . .

. . . can be ugly or out of character.

. . . can lower property values.

. . . increases traffic congestion.

. . . brings pollution and noise to the neighborhood.

. . . can bring crime to the neighborhood.

JUSTICE

An apartment complex . . .

. . . reduces exclusion by economic class, age, family status, etc.

. . . involves less disruption of natural habitat per dwelling than single-family houses.

An apartment complex . . .

. . . creates a class of 'free riders' (renters who benefit from the neighborhood without investing in it).

SUSTAINABILITY

An apartment complex . . .

. . . makes relatively efficient use of energy for climate control and transportation.

An apartment complex . . .

. . . increases demand on municipal services out of proportion to increased revenue.

. . . undermines cultural values of home-ownership and suburban character.

LEGITIMACY

An apartment complex . . .

. . . is a legitimate use of private land, subject to zoning and environmental regulations.

. . . may be part of a regional solution to regional problems.

An apartment complex . . .

. . . is not a legitimate use of private land if it conflicts with local interests.

. . . may have been foisted on the local community by 'outsiders' (e.g., planners, developers).

One way to do this is to be more specific about what we think a particular landscape should be like. If I think it should be a public park in which wildlife habitat takes priority, I should say so explicitly rather than simply demanding more green space. If you would rather see the landscape given over to recreational uses of a particular sort, you should say so as well.[4] Then, at least, we know where we stand and we know more precisely what we need to talk about. We may look for a way to design the park so it can accommodate both sets of values, and maybe some others besides. Or, we could take the issue head-on and consider whether one set of values should be given priority over others in this case. The point is that if we were to stand together in demanding generic green space we might be able to paper over our real differences, but what we would be likely to get is a green space that does not satisfy anyone.

As already noted in the case of proxy battles, we should not be too optimistic about the prospects for solutions that accommodate everyone. Once we get beyond vague agreement or disagreement and delve into the details, we may be faced with much sharper disagreements that are harder to paper over. We may discover that our differences regarding a particular project hinge on differences regarding basic values, their scope, and their relevance to the project. In the case of the apartment building, we may disagree about what justice means and what it implies for issues of affordable housing: Does a community have an obligation to provide affordable housing for a diverse population, or should everyone be left to fend for themselves in the housing market as it now exists? In such cases, the framework serves as a reminder that making decisions about what to build where really does involve matters of ethical inquiry at least as much as matters of economics or politics.

So, if you and I have different views about what justice is and what it requires in a given situation, we should examine our differences more closely, drawing out our own assumptions, acknowledging our biases, and subjecting them all to critical scrutiny. The result of this may not be agreement, but at least we both might learn something from the process. We might come away with a more coherent ethical perspective and a more nuanced understanding of our situation. The idea that our values themselves may be transformed through inquiry is often lacking from disputes that are pitched entirely in economic or political terms.

Disagreement over a project often turns on disagreement or uncertainty about matters of fact. Will a new apartment complex increase traffic congestion, or will that be offset by an increase in walking or transit use? Do apartment buildings necessarily increase criminal activity and decrease property values in the surrounding neighborhoods? These are questions that call for empirical investigation into how a particular place works and how a given project is likely to unfold there. If such an investigation leaves us with some uncertainty, then our deliberation will turn in part on how we think we should respond to that uncertainty.

So far, these suggestions about using the framework to focus discussion have not been very adventurous. They have followed the lines already set down in the previous two sections. I would like to make one further suggestion that involves a modification or, at least, an extension of the framework.

To this point I have treated the framework more or less as a one-dimensional list of questions about value, all of which are in principle of equal importance. In making sense of particular places, though, it would be more helpful to have instead a dynamic and multidimensional model of what might be called the ethical space in which the decision is to be made.[5] The trick will be to consider the values that are at stake as they play themselves out across different scales.

In the case of the apartment building, for example, notice that scale plays a role in debates about legitimacy. The developer may think of the issue mainly in terms of the parcel on which the apartment complex is to be built and the municipal- or county-level government that has jurisdiction over zoning and building permits. Other advocates for the apartment complex may be thinking about the distribution of affordable housing across the region, and there may even be some regional- or state-level mandate regarding the proportion of new construction that should be below some threshold of affordability.[6] Opponents of the apartment complex may be most interested in the impact of the complex on the neighborhood or neighborhoods immediately adjacent to it and on the right of the local community to control its own destiny. Which is the correct scale at which to consider the problem? Can regional solutions to regional problems be made compatible with local solutions to local problems?

A common variation on problems of scale arises when local projects undertaken for sound local reasons have spillover effects at larger scales. So, municipalities compete for commercial development and road construction money in order to increase their own revenue, but this has consequences for neighboring communities and for the region as a whole: redundant services, traffic congestion, the abandonment of older developed areas, and so on.[7] From an ethical point of view, it may be that local decision makers have a responsibility to exercise some reasonable foresight in avoiding these kinds of effects as much as possible. There may also be a telling argument here for some sort of regional authority for addressing regional spillover effects – though, as already noted, the legitimacy of such authorities is often questioned and even curtailed in the interests of local control.

As noted in the second chapter, a simple model for thinking about scale places a given project in the center of a set of concentric rings, each of which is a distinct scale with which the project is concerned and on which it may have some impact. From my point of view as someone pursuing a project, the smallest scale with which I am typically concerned is that of my body and my immediate surroundings, a scale measured in feet (or meters) and in minutes, hours, or days. The largest scale with which I am concerned is that of the geological, ecological and climatic systems of the entire globe, a scale measured in thousands of miles and in centuries, millennia, or eons. In between, depending on the decision, there is my household, my neighborhood, my city, my region, and my country; or the local ecosystem I inhabit (however altered), the watershed, the biome, the continent. Which scales are relevant will depend on the particular problem I am facing.

To get a grip on what this does to the framework, I would borrow an image from hierarchy theory, a fairly recent development in ecology that is built on the importance of choosing the best scale for a particular purpose. The relationship among scales with respect to ecological processes can be pictured as a layer-cake, which ecologists can slice at different angles to make comparisons within and across discrete scales in space and time.[8] Vertical slices compare the same aspects of ecological processes at different scales, while horizontal slices compare different aspects of processes at the same scale, and diagonal slices compare different aspects of processes at different scales.

Building on this metaphor, I propose that ethical inquiry can also be thought of as slicing the layer-cake at different angles.[9] We could make a vertical slice to compare, for example, how a particular conception of justice plays itself out at the local scale and at the regional scale. We could make a horizontal slice to consider how justice and sustainability interrelate at the national level, or how well-being and justice interrelate in a particular neighborhood. We could also cut diagonally through the layers, to connect well-being at the household level with justice at the regional level and sustainability at the national or global level, local sustainability with international justice, and so on.

Thinking of decision making in this way may even help us to get some handle on what is likely to be the biggest problem of scalar mismatch our species has ever faced. With global climate change, we have discovered that local actions to promote well-being are having global spillover effects that threaten national and even local sustainability. Meanwhile, there are issues of international justice as developing nations demand some share of prosperity, and issues of legitimacy at all scales as international bodies, nations, and even individual cities and states have claimed for themselves the authority to decide what to do, if anything, in the face of a global problem. It is safe to say that the situation is exceedingly messy, with a profusion of ethical issues at all scales, wrapped up together with just enough knowledge to spur us to action and just enough uncertainty to give us pause. I hope I have shown, however, that we can use the expanded version of the framework to structure our approach to the problem, at least enough to give us a starting point for deliberation.

5.4. Search for new possibilities

When we think and talk about the built environment, we can easily fall into false dichotomies. One position clashes with another, and we come to think of those positions as the only options available to us. For a variety of political and psychological reasons, we are unwilling or unable to consider other possibilities. We think, for example, that a person must either favor or oppose suburban patterns of development, favor or oppose allowing people to drive wherever they want. Stating the choice in stark, either-or terms can serve the purposes of political rhetoric, of course, especially when the goal is to vilify the opposition: They want more sprawl! or: They want to take away your cars! At a more personal level, the either-or choice can offer some comfort, making it more tolerable to practice resignation: I may be dissatisfied with the landscape that has resulted from suburbanization, but at least it is better than life would have been in an urban tenement slum.

Advocates for the 'new urbanism' or traditional neighborhood design have been important players in public debate about metropolitan growth in the United States. While they might agree that life in the suburbs is in many respects better than life in a tenement slum, they would argue that it is much worse than life in cities and small towns as they would have been before industrialization. The idea of new urbanism is to create new places that capture the very best of what cities and towns have offered in the past, restoring connections among functions in the built environment that have been severed by suburban development patterns.[10] Houses are set close together and close to the street; they have front porches that create a transition between the private space of the home and the public space of the sidewalk. The sidewalk itself can actually serve its traditional function, as there are worthwhile destinations a short walk away in a town square or a main street that serves as a meaningful public space and an economic and civic center of the community at the same time. In short, a new urbanist development is intended to be everything an old American small town would have been, or a Tuscan hill village, or a particularly vibrant neighborhood in an old European city.

For my own part, I have no particular objection to the new urbanist vision of the built environment. At their best, new-urbanist developments like Seaside, Florida, are very appealing, though not without their problems and their detractors.[11] If nothing else, new urbanists and their allies have thought more carefully than many about what makes good places work.

I do have some worries about the way the new urbanist vision is presented, however. It is not hard to get the impression that the American people are confronted by a stark either-or choice: either continue to build disconnected and dispiriting places as we have been doing for the past sixty years, or go back to traditional ways of building from the time before our fall from urban grace. For particularly strident advocates, like James Howard Kunstler, the choice is even more stark: salvation or damnation, civilization or barbarism. In considering the knowledge of how to build coherent neighborhoods, knowledge he sees as being embodied in the new urbanism and traditional neighborhood design, Kunstler asserts: 'we have the ability to restore the dwelling place of our civilization. The more difficult question is: do we have the will to be civilized?'[12]

Now, not all new-urbanist rhetoric is so blunt, and new urbanist planners and builders usually have to be pragmatic, bending their

plans away from a pure vision in order to be able to build in a particular place.[13] Still, the impression remains that new urbanism is
meant to be taken as the one viable alternative to the status quo
– and hence the one truly viable option for human habitation.

Part of this impression comes from before-and-after pictures
that turn up in books, publicity materials, and public presentations
of new-urbanist proposals. The first picture may be of a particularly
chaotic commercial strip in the conventional suburban pattern,
with six or eight lanes of traffic bordered by a jumble of large signs
and vast parking lots, all overhung by criss-crossing wires. The
second picture is the same scene, digitally altered so the connector
road has become a tree-lined boulevard with a wide median and
on-street parking. Shoppers stroll along wide sidewalks lined by
shop windows, buffered from the street by wrought-iron benches
and old-fashioned street lamps as well as the trees and parked
cars. The overhead wires have vanished. The question, implicit or
explicit, is: Would you rather shop *here* or *here*?

This is meant to be a rhetorical question, and the answer is
meant to be obvious: the second picture is self-evidently better.
The problem with rhetorical questions, though, is that the actual
answer given by actual people may come as a surprise. Looking
at the two pictures, I could reasonably respond that, all things
considered, I would rather have the first. Sure, the second picture
looks nice; it reminds me of the fabled Main Street or, depending on the width of the boulevard, the Champs-Elysées. On the
other hand, the shops look like they might be too upscale for my
budget, and it would take a long time and visits to many shops
to find the variety of goods that would be available to me at a
discount in a single big-box retail store. Besides, rather than a
time of innocence and strong community, images of Main Street
might get me thinking of nosy and meddlesome neighbors and
stultifying social conformity. So, given the choice between the
status quo and the idealized new-urban scene, I might find I have
good reason to stick with the status quo, even if I am not very
happy about it.

In some ways, this would be an unfortunate response, mostly because I would be buying into the false dichotomy embodied in the two pictures. In different terms, I would be joining with those presenting the two options in a failure of imagination – a failure, that is, to imagine there might be many other ways of configuring our environment to support our various projects. A better response to the either-or choice might be: Neither. What else have you got to show me?

This is where I think the framework can come into its own as a spur to creativity. Looking beyond the two positions on offer to the complex interests and values that lie hidden beneath, we can start to see and talk about the real advantages and disadvantages of both ways of configuring the landscape. Then we might be able to ask: What else is possible? Can we devise a new configuration, using the means we now have available, to put together a built environment that is unlike anything we have seen before, so it can support our many projects? Is there a way, at least, to make the landscape more diverse so we can pursue many different projects in ways that are just and sustainable?

Ethics here shifts from inquiry to problem solving, with one of the first steps being to reframe the problem.[14] The issue is not really whether or how we can get back to what we once had, or even whether or how to go on doing what we are doing now, but to build new places and recreate old places so they work better all around, given all of our values and all of our projects.

As an aside, there is a further danger in the appeal to compelling images. People may capitalize on nostalgia for Main Street by packaging and selling a kind of pseudo-urbanism: developments that function like the conventional commercial strips in the first image, but which bear a superficial resemblance to the urban charm of the second image. A prominent example of this is what I have come to think of as a fragged mall: a conventional shopping mall built in bits and pieces scattered around a huge parking lot, with an imitation of Main Street at its heart. Many of the visual details are in place, from slight architectural variation among storefronts to old-fashioned street lamps, but the piped-in (piped-out?) music does tend to spoil the effect, as does the absence, in most cases, of actual residents and of public spaces and institutions. It really is just a mall, and not at all the sort of thing new urbanists are after. In order to see this, though, it is necessary to look past the image of Main Street and consider how it functions in relation to real human projects.

Again, I want to be fair to new urbanists, as well as to advocates in the broader 'smart growth' movement. As I have said, they have often gone farther than others in thinking critically and in detail about how places work. In spite of the problem with before-and-after pictures, new urbanists have also gone farther than others to look for creative alternatives to even more pernicious false dichotomies within the domain of conventional development.

Take the case of an old indoor shopping mall that has been abandoned and now stands derelict.[15] By almost any measure, this is a bad thing. The building is an eyesore and a potential threat to the security of surrounding neighborhoods, almost an open invitation to vandalism and crime. It represents the loss of economic opportunity in the short term, but it also represents the long-term problem of economic unsustainability and governmental fragmentation in a rapidly growing metropolis: the mall was abandoned because investment and shoppers went to larger and newer malls a few miles away in other communities.

After a few years, a major big-box retail chain proposes to buy the land and develop it, on the condition they can get the zoning variances they need to convert the existing building and parking lot into a 'giga-center', their largest format for a retail store. People in the community may have hated the mall, but suppose that many of them have no great love of big-box retail in general and of this chain in particular. They worry about the ugliness of the typical giga-center, the increase in traffic congestion, and the economic drain on communities that has resulted when big-box retail stores undermine smaller, locally owned businesses. They also worry the economic benefits to the community will be slight, mostly taking the form of low-wage, dead-end jobs with few benefits.

Local elected officials, who have been working closely with the retail chain, offer their constituents a simple choice: leave things as they are, or go with the proposal from the big-box chain. Surely, they argue, a giga-center is better than an abandoned mall.

This is clearly a false dichotomy, which local residents might see as a devil's bargain. The big-box store, they can argue, is an improvement, of sorts, but only with respect to one or two values – safety and economic opportunity – but it may bring about a degradation with respect to other values – economic and cultural sustainability, and perhaps ecological sustainability as well. The aesthetic value may be a wash, since they may see a big-box store as little better than the abandoned mall. Surely, they might reply, we can do better than this. There must be some way to redevelop the site such that the result would be an improvement along many other dimensions of value as well.

In fact, there have been a number of mall redevelopment projects around the country that have followed, more or less, the principles of new urbanism, turning old indoor malls into mixed-use town centers that serve a number of different public and private functions.[16] So, yes, neighbors might say to their local officials, a big-box giga-center is better than an abandoned mall, but there are many, many things that are better than a big-box giga-center. The matter is at least open to debate.

6. The Limits of Ethics

We often think and speak of our actions in terms of movement along a path towards a goal, drawing metaphorically from the common human experience of moving across a landscape.[1] We pursue projects, work towards our goals. We can arrive at a goal, we can be almost there, or maybe we are just starting out. Along the way, we hope to make good progress. The path can be rocky or smooth; it can be a long, hard climb, or it can be downhill all the way. Understood in these terms, ethical decision making is a matter of being thoughtful in choosing where we want to go and in selecting the best ways to get there, and it is a matter of looking back to evaluate both the wisdom of our choices and the progress we have made. It helps to have a compass, or at least a roadmap.

But a further question arises at this point. To what degree are the journey and the destination within my control, so it is my choices that determine where I end up? In more technical terms, the question is one of responsibility, in two senses (Table 6.1): being responsible as I choose and act, but also being held responsible when my choices and actions go wrong.

Table 6.1

Two Further Ethical Questions
To what extent can people act responsibly?
To what extent can people be held responsible for their actions?

It may be appealing to think there is a clear, unbroken line from intentions to results. In that case, all it would take to be responsible in pursuing a project is to have the right intentions and make the right choices. If I remain true to those choices, I am sure to end up in the right place. From the other side, it would be easy to assign praise or blame. Others have only to see where I end up and ask after the intentions and choices that led me there. If I end up in a bad place, it must be the result of bad choices on my part, and perhaps even bad character. I may be blamed accordingly.

Stated in these terms, the idea of an unbroken line from intention to result, from the decision to set out to my arrival at the destination, may seem terribly naïve. And yet, I suspect this idea still shapes the hopes we have for ourselves and the judgments we make about others. Reading and listening to the rhetoric of those who advocate social change, for example, it sometimes seems their hopes rest precisely on the power of intentions. Once people see the problems of metropolitan growth and understand how they have come about, an advocate might hope, they will start to think differently about their own lives in the world. Once they start to think differently, they will make different choices for themselves and their communities, which will lead directly to changes in their behavior, which will lead directly to changes in the results: better ways of building and living. Raise consciousness, change people's intentions, and the rest follows naturally.

Cutting the other way, the idea of an unbroken line might lead those who advocate change in the status quo to become judgmental: if the patterns of metropolitan growth do not change, then it must be that people are not acting to change the way they live in the landscape, which means they are not making the right choices. If we, the advocates, have informed them of the problems of metropolitan growth and yet they still do not act, then we must conclude that they are bad people, either craven or cowardly.

As it happens, there is little reason to think the line from intention to result is either straight or unbroken. However thoughtful we may be in making our decisions, there is no guarantee we will actually arrive at our chosen destination, or that the destination will turn out to be what we thought or hoped it might be. Again, this is a common human experience that has been folded into the language we use to describe the ways in which projects can be frustrated. We can get bogged down or stopped in our tracks. We can run into a brick wall and, if we are too persistent, waste our time and effort beating our heads against it. We can be diverted, or we can find ourselves at a crossroads, unsure which is the right way to go. From time to time, we may find ourselves at a dead end, discovering that the path we have chosen was never going to lead us where we thought it would and that we can no longer retrace our steps. The road to hell is paved with good intentions. In short, there are all sorts of ways in which we can get stuck on the way to reaching our goals.

The experience of being stuck suggests that the line from intention to result can be broken in any number of places, in which case questions of moral responsibility become much more complicated. People always make decisions within particular situations that present them with a particular set of opportunities and constraints, many of which are beyond the direct control of the decision maker. To the extent the result, the action, and even the decision itself are shaped by those opportunities and constraints, it may be hard to say what it means to choose and act responsibly, and hard to tell to what extent particular people can be held responsible for the result.

This book has been built on the idea that ethical inquiry should play a key role in guiding our decisions about built environment. The account would not be complete without giving some thought to the limits of ethics in actually shaping the built environment and the projects people pursue within it. Notice that this is about the limits of ethics, not the futility of ethics. Where moral responsibility is concerned, the point of thinking about the ways in which people may be constrained in their choices and actions is not to let people entirely off the hook, nor is it to provide ready-made excuses for inaction or for bad results. The point is to make us more modest in what we expect from ourselves and from one another, and to start us looking for ways to learn from the experience of living under constraints as we try to make better decisions.

6.1. To what extent can people act responsibly?

Part of what it means to act responsibly has already been covered in the second chapter, with the question of how a particular project was chosen. To act responsibly is in part to choose responsively, and to choose responsively is not only to think carefully about values and obligations, ends and means, but to have a finely tuned awareness of the place in which the project will unfold.[2] There is more than this to the idea of moral responsibility, though. To act responsibly is also in part to follow through on a decision, to see a project through to its completion. Responsibility in this sense is a moral virtue: other people can count on a responsible person to stay on course, with both eyes on the goal and a steady hand on the tiller, avoiding diversions and ignoring distractions.

Stated in these terms, the virtue of responsibility requires a great deal of self-control and at least some degree of control over the situation in which a project is to unfold. As it happens, we often have only a little control over the situations in which we find ourselves. Worse, we do not seem to have complete control over ourselves. It is not just that the situations we are in make it difficult to complete the projects we choose to pursue, but they can make it difficult to choose those projects in the first place. We ourselves – our moral understanding, our values, our character – have been shaped by our situation, conditioned to see things and respond to them in particular ways. As Margaret Urban Walker puts it, human agency is 'impure' in the sense that there is not in all instances a single, sharp distinction between the

Table 6.2

Three Kinds of Constraint

---

limits of efficacy: well-chosen projects get stopped or go awry

limits of integrity: conflicting motivations and commitments make it difficult or impossible to choose well

limits of autonomy: moral understanding and moral values are constrained in advance, in ways that are often unnoticed

---

will of the agent and the workings of other causal forces. Because human agency is always situated in particular causal contexts, she argues, it is always impure.[3] If this is the case, then the problem of constraint extends to the way we make decisions, not just to our efforts to carry out the resulting projects.

To put this in different terms, the idealized line that runs from intention to result can be broken in at least three different places (Table 6.2).

Suppose a well-chosen project goes badly awry: action in a particular direction turns out to be impossible, or the results of an action depart wildly from what was expected, perhaps even defeating the purpose of the project itself. In that case, there has been a break in the line somewhere between the action and the result. I refer to such cases as 'limits of efficacy'.

There can also be a break just around the point where the decision is made. When enduring motivations or commitments come into conflict, it can be difficult or impossible to make a decision. Sometimes these are run-of-the-mill moral dilemmas that can be resolved by further reflection and maybe by some creative problem solving. However, there may be internal conflicts that defy resolution. I refer to such persistent conflicts as 'limits of integrity'.

Finally, there may be a break at the very beginning of the line, with the intentions that are supposed to be the root from which the project springs. The idea of autonomy presupposes that moral agents have control over their own minds, if nothing else; we should be able to rearrange our motivations at will. If our character and our understanding are shaped by our relationship with our environment, then some of the roots of our choices are likely to be constrained by forces beyond our control. What makes this especially tricky is that we may be entirely unaware of the ways in which we are constrained. I refer to such constraints as 'limits of autonomy'.

I will get back to each of these three kinds of constraint in a moment. Before I do, I should say again that recognizing the limits of ethics does not make the virtue of moral responsibility any less important. What it does is to add a further dimension to the idea of responsibility, one that is missing in the image of a steady hand on the tiller and eyes locked on the far horizon: to be responsible is in part to be responsive to what actually happens and to the ways in which circumstances and even luck shape our moral lives.[4]

(a) Limits of efficacy

There are some things that human beings cannot do, no matter how hard we try. This is not always a bad thing: our capacities and our limitations as earthbound mammals are what give shape and meaning to our experience. We cannot walk through walls, or fly around by flapping our arms, or see in the ultraviolet, or live without an atmosphere – to take a few obvious examples. We can walk across a relatively level landscape, scramble over some obstacles, grab things with our hands, and so on. Learning to be a human being in the world is, in part, a matter of learning what we can and cannot do given the relationship between our bodies and our environment.

Because we are tool users, though, learning to be a human being is also a matter of learning how to rearrange some aspects of the relationship between our bodies and our environment in order to expand our capacities, we hope without getting our-selves killed. We still cannot walk through walls, but we can make doors that open and close; we cannot live without an atmosphere, but we can make scuba gear and space suits to take some atmos-phere with us into otherwise inhospitable places. In developing technical means to our various ends we do not overcome all limits, however. We just change the configuration of opportunities and constraints, and with them some part of the meaning of human life in the world, sometimes in unexpected ways.

A further wrinkle in understanding the limits of efficacy is that our environment is complex and dynamic, so it may be very difficult to figure out what is possible and what is not possible in a given situation. This may be especially true of the built environment, which is a product of the intertwining of natural, social, and technological dynamics. The shape of a given place in the built environment may be hard to fathom, and there may be some nasty surprises. A project may have the necessary technical means but run up against an economic obstacle, or it may have the economic means but run up against a cultural or political obstacle, or it may have all of its technical and social means lined up just in time for the entire socio-technical system to run up against an underlying natural obstacle. For that matter, a project can defeat itself by changing the shape of the place in which it is to be pursued, throwing up obstacles in its own path.

Suppose that after careful deliberation I decide that walking to work would be a good thing to do, mostly because it would improve my own health and contribute to a reduction in fossil fuel consumption, air pollution, and traffic congestion in my region. Unfortunately, my place of work is a long way from home and I cannot walk from here to there in a straight line: I am constrained to use the existing infrastructure, however convoluted it may be, because I am dependent on that infrastructure to get me across streams and highways, and because I am not allowed to walk across property belonging to others. The best route may include busy roads with no sidewalks, which constrain me to breathing exhaust fumes and exposing myself to the risk of being struck by a car. I may also run into bad luck: on the day I first set out to walk, a key bridge on my route may be closed for construction, or there may be thunderstorms with torrential rain, cloud-to-ground lightning, and the risk of flash floods.

My experience could lead me to conclude that, for practical purposes, my current situation makes it impossible for me to walk to work, even if I am still convinced it is the right thing to do. I could also conclude that I should try to change my circumstances, either moving closer to work or finding a job closer to home. This more ambitious project can also run into trouble given the broader situation in my region. Because of zoning restrictions and the existing patterns of development they have produced, my place of work may be separated from any residential areas by the same kinds of barriers, even if there are neighborhoods closer than the one I live in now. If there are residential areas near to where I work, they may be too expensive for my budget, or too far from other things I want or need. If I try to go the other way, I might find that zoning restrictions, existing infrastructure, economic conditions, as well as my own skills and employment history will block me from finding a job close enough to my current home to make a difference in how I get there.

Now suppose there are lots of other people whose various projects have been frustrated by the current patterns of infrastructure and development in the region. Suppose, for the sake of argument, that there is a broad consensus that basic changes are needed so it will be easier for people to work, shop, and play close to home with an infrastructure that supports walking and cycling. Further suppose, also for the sake of argument, that the concrete proposals emerging from this consensus are well considered, broadly supported, and founded in the best of intentions towards the well-being of the public. Such large-scale political projects can also get stuck in the details of the built environment, even setting aside political opposition from dissenting groups and from powerful vested interests. If nothing else, the existing infrastructure is both hard and heavy. Reconfiguring some part of the landscape to serve some new set of purposes will cost a great deal of time, money, effort, material, and energy: tearing up roads here, putting down new roads there, demolishing and moving buildings along the way.

In real life, of course, it is almost never the case that a large-scale project can proceed on the basis of a broad consensus in the absence of political opposition. People usually disagree with one another and often get in one another's way. Those who have some measure of political or economic power can use it to maintain the circumstances that have given them that power, blocking or diverting projects that might shake things up. Beyond the hurly-burly of the political process, there is also the problem of inertia: the institutions that support current ways of building – real estate markets, government agencies, engineering schools, and so on – may be slow to respond to calls for change simply because they are human institutions with a stake in their own stability.

In relation to the limits of efficacy, acting responsibly seems to be a matter of paying attention to the details of our environment, in all of its complexity. We should use foresight in planning our projects, learning the lie of the land, taking into account what we know of circumstances beyond our control that may help or hinder us. We should also be prepared for surprises along the way, and we should be reasonably persistent in the face of opposition. At some point, when a project fails or just before, being responsible may mean stopping and going back, re-examining the situation, reconsidering means and ends, and maybe even questioning basic perceptions and motivations before starting out again, perhaps on some new course towards some more modest goal.

(b) Limits of integrity

The interesting thing about my example of trying to walk to work is that I seem to bump up against a conflict among my own motivations and commitments. Suppose, on the one hand, I am deeply committed to the idea that physical activity should be a regular part of my daily routine, in part for the sake of my own health, in part for the sake of energy efficiency and sustainability. But suppose, on the other hand, I have a range of other deep commitments that pull in other directions, given current circumstances: I seek to maximize the amount of time I can spend with my family and I seek to maximize the amount of time I can spend at work, which push me to minimize the amount I spend moving back and forth between them. I seem to be in a bind.

There may be any number of ways to get out of such a bind. On reflection, I may decide that one commitment is more important than the others. I may also try, with a little creativity, to change my circumstances so I can meet all of these commitments at once, subject to the limits of efficacy. I may even settle for a compromise among the various commitments, not really meeting any of them fully, but not entirely violating them either. These are all possible ways of dealing with practical dilemmas.

Some dilemmas may cut a little deeper, to the point they undermine the integrity of the person who is trying to make a decision. I understand integrity to be a moral virtue, an admirable character trait that suggests a wholeness or unity among the value judgments, habits, inclinations, and commitments of an individual. For someone with integrity, all motivations pull in more or less the same direction, towards the same goals. The lifelong project of becoming a whole person can be thought of as a process of integration, a process that may or may not go smoothly.

The problem we often face is that character formation starts early, generally before we can exercise any direct control over the process. By the time we come to full consciousness, many of our values and motivations have already been shaped and set by our upbringing, our circumstances, and maybe even by our genes. When we are paying attention, we may find that commitments that are deeply entrenched in our character pull against one another and against new commitments that we have since taken on by choice.

At the farthest extreme, feminist scholars have pointed out that conditions of oppression can make the development and maintenance of integrity all but impossible. A woman who grows up in a society that assumes the inferiority and subservience of women may come to internalize those assumptions, which she experiences as a basic inclination towards submissiveness. If she later becomes a feminist and commits herself to the principle that women are equal to men, she will not automatically cancel out her older inclination. More likely, she will experience a conflict as her older tendency towards submissiveness resists change.[5]

Where the built environment is concerned, it would be going too far to say that conflicting motivations are the product of out-right oppression. Even so, individual decision makers may find they have acquired strong and persistent inclinations towards particular patterns of development that they have subsequently come to judge as bad. Suppose I come to be committed to the idea that mixed-use and mixed-income communities are really the best places to live, but I still feel in my bones that single-use residential developments that are strictly segregated by class are the only way to guarantee financial and personal security, simply because that is all I have ever experienced. What would be the responsible course of action in such a circumstance?

Where the limits of integrity are concerned, being respon-sible seems to require some degree of self-knowledge. At the very least, we should attend to tensions and conflicts that arise among our own motivations, and we should do what we can to trace those tensions back to their roots. When we take on new commitments, we should be willing to engage in the long and difficult struggle to hold to those new commitments even in the face of the pressure exerted by older commitments. We should be modest in what we expect of ourselves, however, and in what we expect of one another. As the feminist scholar Lisa Tessman puts it, personal transformation is no easy thing: 'one cannot simply will one's character to change'.[6]

(c) Limits of autonomy

Back in the first chapter, I noted the importance of choice in eval-uating the moral worth of a project. The question was not only *how* the project was chosen, but *whether* it was chosen. But what does it mean to choose or, more to the point, to choose freely?

Moral autonomy (literally self-rule) is a central concept in philosophical ethics, particularly in the tradition that stems from Rousseau and Kant. As a moral agent, I am autonomous to the extent I am governed by a law I make for myself. That is to say, I am autonomous to the extent I am capable of making unconstrained choices on the basis of my own reasoning about what is good and what is right. It is essential to this view of ethics that the actions of moral beings are not determined by outside forces, whether in the form of social pressure or of natural inclinations.[7]

But can human choices really be so unconstrained? Just how autonomous can we be?

To see how human autonomy might be limited, consider a twist on the limits of integrity. Suppose I have a deep-seated commitment to living in a particular kind of neighborhood, a commitment shaped by my upbringing and reinforced by the investments I have already made. Further suppose I have never had any reason to question my commitment, so I am effectively unaware that I have it. As far as I am concerned, the kind of neighborhood I prefer is simply the proper setting for a human life, and I cannot imagine how anyone could manage to live anywhere else. This commitment constrains in advance any decisions I make about where to live and about how I should respond to proposed changes in the built environment, and this constraint amounts to a limitation on my autonomy. When I make a decision under the constraints imposed by a prior commitment of this sort, some viable options have already been taken off the table without my knowledge or my consent.

The uncomfortable truth here is that, in spite of Kantian hopes for human rationality, we seem to run up against such limits of autonomy all the time, though they may have different sources. Some limits come from inside ourselves, some come from outside. What they have in common is that, unlike limits of integrity that we experience as overt moral dilemmas, we can become aware of the limits of autonomy only in hindsight, through a difficult process of critical inquiry that usually requires the help of other people.

A prior commitment to living in a particular kind of neighborhood can serve as an example of a limit that comes from inside, at least to the extent it is a matter of perception and cognition. As I discussed in the first chapter, we humans live in a world of infinite detail, but our ability to pay attention to detail is necessarily finite. In order to avoid being overwhelmed, we filter out all but a fairly narrow range of what the world throws at us. A lot of this work is done by the sensory and perceptual apparatus we inherit as members of our species, which have been tuned by natural selection to take in sensory information within the narrow range of what is most relevant to our survival and to shape it in particular ways. We tend to pay attention to things that are about the size of things we can eat and things that can eat us, for example, but exclude systems and cycles that are too big and slow or too small and fast to be immediately relevant.

Even within the narrower range of what we are equipped to perceive, we have to make sense of a great deal of detail. We do this, cognitive scientists tell us, by *making* sense of it: we filter the detail through mental models or conceptual schemata to sort out what is important and what is not. These conceptual schemata constitute the world of our experience; in a sense, they *are* the world of our experience. Without them, we might be said not to really experience anything at all.

It is important to understand that there is not just one conceptual schema shared universally among all human beings. Rather, as noted in the first chapter, schemata are as diverse as they are partial and selective; in fact, they often diverge sharply from one another. The diversity and partialness of schemata implies there is never a unique, correct, literal description of a situation that calls for a moral response. Instead, as Mark Johnson notes, 'there are multiple possible framings of any given situation, and hence different moral consequences depending on which way we frame the situation'.[8] Think, for example, of the two hypothetical people mentioned in the Introduction, who see the same urban street-scape differently: one sees a vibrant civic and cultural life while another person sees only filth and the possibility of getting mugged. It seems that the two are making sense of the scene through different cognitive filters. As a consequence, they can be expected to make very different private choices about where to live and to have very different responses to public decisions about investing – or not – in urban revitalization.

The question concerning autonomy is whether and to what extent any of us has control over the filters we use when making sense of the world. It could be argued that we are truly autono-mous only to the extent we do have such control – which does not augur well for autonomy. By the time we come to awareness of ourselves as moral beings and start to make choices for our-selves, we already have a stock of conceptual schemata we have acquired from our culture, from the particular choices of those who came before us, from our own early experiences, and so on, all bounded by our perceptual capacities as human beings. As difficult as it is for any one of us to change our character when we are aware of conflicts among commitments and motivations, it is likely to be still more difficult to change the way we perceive the world.

There may be a way in which the built environment itself can shape our perceptions and our expectations from the outside. One approach to the study of technology and society, called actor-network theory, has it that the social and technological world we inhabit is the product of a complex struggle among various actors, including artifacts and institutions as well as individual people. All along the way, human actors inscribe non-human actors (artifacts, that is) with particular meanings and particular ways of channeling human effort. Those non-human actors in turn prescribe certain behaviors to the human actors who interact with them. Bruno Latour describes this in terms of delegating moral responsibilities to artifacts. A hydraulic door-closer, to take one of Latour's examples, imposes an energy tax on everyone who pushes the door open, in order to be more competent and more rigorous in enforcing its program for proper social conduct: 'Close the door!'[9] To the extent the whole of the built environment can be thought of as a socio-technical ensemble, as I suggested in the third chapter, it is full of such scripts: the way the landscape is divided up and zoned, the way streets are laid out and built, the presence or absence of sidewalks, and so on and on.

It may well be that the scripts inscribed in the landscape are originally written by humans, but not necessarily by any one human. To the extent socio-technical ensembles are the product of a struggle among human and non-human actors, any one individual could never exercise direct or complete control over the process of delegating responsibilities to non-human actors. As a consequence, the built environment may well come to prescribe ways of acting that are experienced as alien by any given individual choosing and acting within it.

The role of scripts in shaping human behavior is already a challenge to autonomy, but a still more serious challenge arises because many scripts are hidden from awareness. We may grow up with scripts that are already firmly inscribed in the landscape, or we may quickly become accustomed to new scripts, so we take them for granted as natural and inevitable.[10] In other words, we internalize some scripts, making them an integral part of the conceptual filters by which we make sense of the world. The result of all of this is that individuals living within a given built environment may find it very difficult to determine when they are writing their own scripts – acting autonomously – and when they are merely reading off scripts that have been presented to them for no particular reason by no one in particular.

The very idea of moral responsibility is up against the ropes here. It does not seem possible to choose and act responsibly if the roots of our choices are out of sight and out of reach. If we are to have any hope of acting responsibly, it seems we have to do what we can to unearth these roots, to discover and trace the history of the limitations of the various filters we use to make sense of the world. To the extent we are successful in doing this, we may at least be able to turn limits of autonomy into ordinary limits of integrity – explicit conflicts among motivations and commitments – so we can carry on the struggle from there.

The real difficulty in doing this is precisely that we are usually unaware of the filters we use to shape our awareness of the world. At first, the limits of autonomy may only be apparent from the viewpoint of other people. To take an extreme example, think of the audience of an ancient tragedy, watching the hero walk with blithe self-assurance towards destruction. Oedipus was missing something, unable to pay attention to certain crucial aspects of his own situation. He was too bold in calling down curses that ended up falling on his own head. The compelling drama of the story is that the audience can see plainly the error of which Oedipus is unaware until it is too late. In less dramatic settings, it may be that we can become aware of the limits of our own autonomy through a process of critical inquiry that we pursue together with others, particularly with people who see things differently than we do and so may see us more clearly than we see ourselves.

We may also be able to stumble across evidence of our own limits on our own, if only in hindsight, assuming we are continually asking critical questions about our own actions, the motives behind them, and the ways they played themselves out in our environmental context. Looking back on the course of our own lives, we may be able to see that we have missed something we might better have paid attention to, that our options had been artificially narrowed, our autonomy constrained.

If we were to continue this inquiry into our own motives, as constraint after constraint is brought to light, it may occur to us that there is no reason to suppose our current understanding of the world is the final and best one. The result would be a kind of ethical modesty that is rooted in an acknowledgement of the limits of human cognition: given the kinds of beings we are, there are likely always to be still more constraints on our autonomy that may come to light later on. To be morally responsible, then, is to be mindful of our fallibility and cautious in what we claim for ourselves.

6.2. To what extent can people be held responsible for their actions?

The flip-side of being responsible for our own actions is holding people responsible for their actions. When we come across something good or bad in our environment, we often want to trace it back to particular people so we can single them out for praise or blame. Suppose a project goes horribly wrong. We want to know: Whose fault is it? The hope is that we can follow the path backward from result to action, from action to choice, from choice to intention, from intention to character, which we might then take to be the root of the problem. In other words, we sometimes think as though bad situations are always brought about by bad people.

It turns out that holding people responsible is just as complicated as being responsible, and for many of the same reasons. Suppose a group of people finds a particular state of affairs to be intolerably bad – the early industrial city, for example, or twenty-first-century freeway sprawl. It might be comforting to be able to point fingers at some other group of people – 'them' – who can be held responsible for that state of affairs, a cabal of powerful special interests, perhaps, or people of a particular social class. This has the advantage of letting 'us' off the hook: What could we do in the face of such power or such devilry?

The problem is that the built environment is far too complex and diverse to have been shaped by any one group of people, however powerful they may be. Instead, it has been formed by countless choices and actions taken by countless groups and individuals – including 'us' – and the whole has turned out to be more than the sum of those choices and actions. It is a system, and sometimes the interactions among the various components come as a surprise even to the best-informed observers. One consequence of this is that praise or blame for the resulting state of affairs would have to be distributed widely. This is not to say it would have to be distributed equally, as some groups may really have had more influence on the shape of the built environment than others, but it would still be inappropriate to single out one group for all the blame. More to the point, praise or blame would have to be filtered and mitigated by our recognition of the various breaks in the chain that runs from intention to action to result.

It is a convention in ethics as in law that people should only be praised or blamed, rewarded or punished, for outcomes over which they have control. A child might be held blameless for an action that would call for severe punishment if it were carried out by an adult, on the assumption that the child is not yet developed enough to be fully autonomous. Any number of factors might be seen to limit autonomy and so to mitigate guilt, including coercion, mental illness, ignorance, or other impairments. There are also other ways in which people might do bad things or bring about bad results without being bad people with bad intentions. They may labor under the limits of integrity, confused about their intentions and unsure how to reconcile conflicting motivations. They may meet with the limits of efficacy, acting on good intentions only to have them backfire because of some hidden obstacle in their environment.

It is not my goal to provide people with a universal excuse, a sort of moral blank check they can use to avoid being blamed for their actions. There are certainly situations in which praise or blame would be appropriate, however they may be mitigated by circumstances. Each of us should be willing to accept blame for actions over which we do have control and, in the interest of modesty, to deflect praise for actions over which we do not.

In either case, the degree of praise or blame should be matched as precisely as possible to the degree of control, and we should make allowances for one another given our limits and the complexity of the situations in which we have to choose and act. Given that we are all impure agents, Tessman argues, we should cultivate the virtue of compassion, which 'helps one to not assign *too* much responsibility (to oneself or others) when it is not deserved. It helps one to say, "this is the best I (or she, or he) can do under the circumstances of bad luck".'[11] Compassion works as a kind of modesty or grace in relationships with others, and feeds into the civic virtues of tolerance and openness to critical discourse.

In the end, though, I am just not much interested in the question of praise or blame. I do not take it to be as important to the project of ethical inquiry as the question of what it means to act responsibly. More than this, undue fixation on assigning blame is generally unproductive: not only do we waste time and energy in the public forum on endless finger-pointing, but those who are quickest to point fingers at others may be slowest to learn, since they are often unwilling or unable to admit or examine their own limitations and their own failures to choose and act responsibly. The time and energy now spent pointing fingers at one another would be better spent working out how we can make better decisions together about the places where we live.

Notes

1. Ethics

1. Patricia Hogue Werhane *Moral Imagination and Management Decision-making,* New York: Oxford University Press, 1999, pp. 49–50.
2. Mark Johnson *Moral Imagination: Implications of Cognitive Science for Ethics,* Chicago: University of Chicago Press, 1993, pp. 8–9.
3. Michael J. Pardales '"So, How Did You Arrive at that Decision?" Connecting Moral Imagination and Moral Judgment', *Journal of Moral Education* 2002, 31, 403–32.
4. Anthony Weston makes a similar point in terms of three 'families' of values: goods, rights, and virtues; see Anthony Weston *A 21st Century Ethical Toolbox,* Oxford: Oxford University Press, 2001, pp. 68–75. As for the theories of philosophical ethics, there are other possibilities than the 'big three' outlined here; for an excellent overview, see James Rachels *The Elements of Moral Philosophy,* 4th edn, Boston, MA: McGraw-Hill, 2003.
5. Aristotle *The Nicomachean Ethics*, trans. H. Rackham, The Loeb Classic Library, ed. G. P. Goold, revised edn, vol. XIX, Cambridge, MA and London: Harvard University Press and William Heinemann Ltd, 1934, II.v–vi. (1105b17–07a8).
6. Sometimes translated 'prudence'. See Aristotle, *The Nicomachean Ethics*, VI.ix. (1142a32–43a18).
7. Immanuel Kant *Groundwork of the Metaphysics of Morals*, trans. H. J. Paton, New York: Harper Torchbooks, 1958, pp. 95–6 (Ak.427–9).
8. John Stuart Mill *Utilitarianism,* Indianapolis: Hackett, 1979, p. 7.
9. Aristotle *The Nicomachean Ethics*, I.i. (1094a1–18).

10. Aristotle *The Nicomachean Ethics*, I.vii.1–16. (1097a15–98a20).

11. In Kant's own terms, will stands opposed to 'inclinations'. Regarding the function of reason, see Kant, *Groundwork*, pp. 62–4 (Ak.394–6).

12. Mill, *Utilitarianism*, pp. 16–17, 23–4.

13. This metaphor is the root of Plato's conception of justice in the polis; see Plato, 'Republic', trans. Paul Shorey, *The Collected Dialogues of Plato*, eds Edith Hamilton and Huntington Cairns, Princeton, NJ: Princeton University Press, 1961, 368c–e, 462a. The idea of organic unity in the state has its echoes in the work of Hobbes and Rousseau: Thomas Hobbes *Leviathan*, New York: Penguin, 1968 (1651), pp. 227–8; Jean-Jacques Rousseau *The Social Contract and other later political writings*, trans. Victor Gourevitch, *Cambridge Texts in the History of Political Thought*, eds Raymond Guess and Quentin Skinner, Cambridge: Cambridge University Press, 1997, p. 121.

14. See John Rawls *Justice as Fairness: A Restatement,* Cambridge, MA: Harvard/Belknap, 2001, p. 9.

2. Ethics and Environment

1. Andrew Light 'The Urban Blind Spot in Environmental Ethics', *Environmental Politics* 2001, 10.1, 17.

2. Thoreau's declaration is in his essay, 'Walking'. See Henry David Thoreau *The Natural History Essays,* Salt Lake City: Peregrine Smith, 1980, p. 122.

3. Aldo Leopold *A Sand County Almanac and Sketches Here and There,* New York: Oxford University Press, 1949, p. 204.

4. Robert P. McIntosh 'Pluralism in Ecology', *Annual Review of Ecology and Systematics* 1987, 18, 321; Daniel B. Botkin *Discordant Harmonies: A New Ecology for the Twenty-First Century,* Oxford: Oxford University Press, 1990, pp. 12–13.

5. Light 'The Urban Blind Spot in Environmental Ethics', 7–8. See also Robert Kirkman 'Reasons to Dwell On (if Not Necessarily In) the Suburbs', *Environmental Ethics* 2004, 26.1, 80.

6. See James J. Gibson *The Ecological Approach to Visual Perception,* Hillsdale, NJ: Lawrence Erlbaum Associates, 1986, p. 127. Gibson proposes a theory of affordances as part of a general account of how

living organisms perceive their environment; affordances can be positive (opportunities) or negative (constraints).

7. Existential phenomenologist Maurice Merleau-Ponty wrote that projects 'polarize the world' of the perceiver, aligning the meaning of experience in a particular way. The implication here is that a new project in effect re-polarizes the world, aligning experience in some different way. Maurice Merleau-Ponty *Phenomenology of Perception*, trans. Colin Smith, London: Routledge, 1962, p. 112.

8. Or so I have argued elsewhere: Robert Kirkman *Skeptical Environmentalism: The Limits of Philosophy and Science*, Bloomington: Indiana University Press, 2002, pp. 151–2.

9. Consciousness, writes Merleau-Ponty, 'is in the first place not a matter of "I think" but of "I can"'. Merleau-Ponty *Phenomenology of Perception*, p. 137.

10. Leopold *A Sand County Almanac*, pp. 205–6.

11. Adapted from Bryan G. Norton *Searching for Sustainability: Interdisciplinary Essays in the Philosophy of Conservation Biology*, Cambridge Studies in Philosophy and Biology, ed. Michael Ruse, Cambridge: Cambridge University Press, 2003, pp. 68–9. See Robert Kirkman 'Ethics and Scale in the Built Environment', *Environmental Philosophy* 2005, 2, 38–52.

12. Timothy F. H. Allen and Thomas W. Hoekstra *Toward a Unified Ecology*, New York: Columbia University Press, 1992, pp. 19–20, 29; Norton *Searching for Sustainability*, p. 67.

13. Leopold *A Sand County Almanac*, pp. 215–16.

14. National Invasive Species Information Center *European Starling*, 6 January 2009. Available: http://www.invasivespeciesinfo.gov/animals/eurostarling.shtml, 12 February 2009.

15. For both an analysis and an example of bias in the debate over 'induced traffic', see Robert Bruegmann *Sprawl: A Compact History*, Chicago: University of Chicago Press, 2005, pp. 129–32.

16. This is a standard account of the character of scientific theory. See Carl Hempel *The Philosophy of Natural Science*, Upper Saddle River, NJ: Prentice-Hall, 1966, pp. 70–2. From a very different tradition, Merleau-Ponty writes of these as the 'hinges' or 'pivots' on which experience turns, but which are themselves hidden in the depths of the world; see Maurice Merleau-Ponty *The Visible and the Invisible*,

trans. Alphonso Lingis, ed. Claude Lefort, Evanston, IL: Northwestern University Press, 1968, pp. 225–6.

17. This is in the spirit of skepticism, which is widely supposed to be a hallmark of the sciences. Eighteenth-century skeptic David Hume would say that, however good and useful our models might become, the 'ultimate springs and principles' of nature remain hidden. David Hume *Enquiries Concerning Human Understanding and Concerning the Principles of Morals*, eds L. A. Selby-Bigge and P. H. Nidditch, 3rd edn, Oxford: Oxford University Press, 1975, p. 30.

18. There are many versions of this argument. One that comes from the tradition of European phenomenology can be found in Edmund Husserl *The Crisis of European Sciences and Transcendental Phenomenology*, trans. David Carr, Evanston, IL: Northwestern University Press, 1970, see especially pp. 48–9. The critique of the sciences has also been of great interest to environmentalists and environmental philosophers. For just one example among many, see Carolyn Merchant *The Death of Nature: Women, Ecology, and the Scientific Revolution*, New York: Harper and Row, 1980, pp. 290–5.

19. Reports from the Intergovernmental Panel on Climate Change (IPCC) include three different ways of describing uncertainty, each appropriate to a particular context. Assessments in contexts involving statistical analysis employ the language of 'likelihood': 'virtually certain' describes a probability over 99 per cent, 'very likely' describes a probability of 90–99 per cent, 'likely' describes a probability of 66–90 per cent, and so on. See IPCC *Climate Change 2007: Synthesis Report. Contribution of Working Groups I, II and III to the Fourth Assessment Report of the Intergovernmental Panel on Climate Change*, Geneva, Switzerland: IPCC, 2007, p. 27.

20. For a discussion of these options in terms of two types of statistical error, see K. S. Shrader-Frechette and E. D. McCoy *Method in Ecology: Strategies for Conservation*, Cambridge: Cambridge University Press, 1993, pp. 155–6.

21. Then again, it is often those who are most optimistic who cast the debate in these terms. See Bjørn Lomborg *The Skeptical Environmentalist: Measuring the Real State of the World*, Cambridge: Cambridge University Press, 2001, p. 3.

22. Lomborg, for example, claims to counter pessimism with 'the facts',

but his telling of the facts is distinctly colored by his own basic opti-
mism; see Lomborg *The Skeptical Environmentalist*. See also Robert
Kirkman 'Review of *The Skeptical Environmentalist: Measuring the Real
State of the World*', *Environmental Ethics* 2003, 25, 423–6.

3. Metropolitan Growth

1. The U.S. Department of Housing and Urban Development and the
   Census Bureau of the U.S. Department of Commerce make this
   explicit in the *American Housing Survey* (AHS): 'Suburbs are defined
   in the AHS as the portion of each metropolitan area that is not in any
   central city.' U.S. Department of Housing and Urban Development
   and U.S. Department of Commerce *American Housing Survey for the
   United States: 2007,* Washington, D.C., 2008, p. A-28.
2. A number of scholars have attempted to define 'suburb' in this
   narrower sense, with varying degrees of success. See, for example,
   Kenneth T. Jackson *Crabgrass Frontier: The Suburbanization of the
   United States,* Oxford: Oxford University Press, 1985, pp. 4–5; J. John
   Palen *The Suburbs,* New York: McGraw-Hill, 1995, pp. 12–13; Mark
   Baldassare 'Suburban Communities', *Annual Review of Sociology*
   1992, 18 476.
3. Robert Fishman *Bourgeois Utopias: The Rise and Fall of Suburbia,* New
   York: Basic Books, 1987, pp. 51–63.
4. Riverside Improvement Company *Riverside in 1871: With a Description
   of its Improvements, Together with some Engravings of Views and
   Buildings,* Chicago: D. & C. H. Blakely, 1871, p. 21.
5. Mark Baldassare distinguishes four phases of suburbanization from
   the pre-industrial to the metropolitan; residential suburbs in the
   narrow sense arose in the third phase, the late urban-industrial era.
   Baldassare 'Suburban Communities', 476–7.
6. For a definition of sprawl-as-process, see Robert W. Burchell *et al. The
   Costs of Sprawl - 2000*, Transit Cooperative Research Program, vol.
   74, Washington, D.C.: National Academy Press, 2002, pp. 58–9. For a
   definition of sprawl-as-product, see George Galster *et al.* 'Wrestling
   Sprawl to the Ground: Defining and Measuring an Elusive Concept',
   Housing Facts and Findings 2.4 (2000).

7. Sierra Club *Smart Choices or Sprawling Growth: A 50-State Survey of Development,* San Francisco: Sierra Club, 2000, p. 2.

8. Wiebe E. Bijker 'Sociohistorical Technology Studies', *Handbook of Science and Technology Studies*, eds Sheila Jasanoff, Gerald E. Markle, James C. Petersen and Trevor Pinch, Thousand Oaks, CA: Sage Publications, 1995, pp. 229–56; see also Thomas P. Hughes 'The Seamless Web: Technology, Science, Etcetera, Etcetera', *Social Studies of Science* 1986, 16.2, 281–92; Thomas P. Hughes 'The Evolution of Large Technological Systems', *The Social Construction of Technological Systems: New Directions in the Sociology and History of Technology*, eds Wiebe E. Bijker, Thomas P. Hughes and Trevor J. Pinch, Cambridge, MA: MIT Press, 1987, pp. 51–82.

9. John R. Stilgoe *Borderland: Origins of the American Suburb, 1820-1939,* New Haven: Yale University Press, 1988, pp. 28–30; Jackson *Crabgrass Frontier*, pp. 73–81.

10. Oliver Gillham *The Limitless City: A Primer on the Urban Sprawl Debate,* Washington, D.C.: Island Press, 2002, pp. 208–9; Jackson *Crabgrass Frontier*, pp. 168–71.

11. Jane Jacobs *The Death and Life of Great American Cities,* New York: Vintage Books, 1992, pp. 24–5. See also Jackson *Crabgrass Frontier*, pp. 229–30.

12. Jackson *Crabgrass Frontier*, p. 207ff.

13. Recounted in Jackson *Crabgrass Frontier*, p. 209.

14. Gillham *The Limitless City*, pp. 137–8; Angel O. Torres *et al.* 'Closed Doors: Persistent Barriers to Fair Housing', *Sprawl City: Race, Politics, and Planning in Atlanta*, eds Robert D. Bullard, Glenn S. Johnson and Angel O. Torres, Washington, D.C.: Island Press, 2000, pp. 101–6.

15. Rosalyn Baxandall and Elizabeth Ewen *Picture Windows: How the Suburbs Happened,* New York: Basic Books, 2000, pp. 125–7; Jackson *Crabgrass Frontier*, pp. 234–8.

4. The Ethics of Metropolitan Growth

1. I have been developing this framework gradually over a period of several years. It really began to take shape in 2003, after a summer of empirical research in and around Atlanta, Georgia, including

interviews with professionals, academics, public officials, and activists whose work draws them into debates about metropolitan growth. The empirical research was funded by a Summer Stipend from the National Endowment for the Humanities. See Robert Kirkman 'The Ethics of Metropolitan Growth: A Framework', *Philosophy & Geography* 2004, 7.2, 201–18.

2. See Reid Ewing *et al.* 'Relationship Between Urban Sprawl and Physical Activity, Obesity, and Morbidity', *American Journal of Health Promotion* 2003, 18.1, 47–57.

3. Chauncey Starr 'Social Benefit Versus Technological Risk', *Science* 1969, 165.3899, 1235–7.

4. Tavia Simmons and Grace O'Neill 'Households and Families: 2000', Washington, D.C.: U.S. Census Bureau, 2001, p. 2.

5. Andres Duany *et al. Suburban Nation: The Rise of Sprawl and the Decline of the American Dream,* New York: North Point Press, 2000, pp. 116–17.

6. Robert D. Putnam *Bowling Alone: The Collapse and Revival of American Community,* New York: Simon and Schuster, 2000, p. 19.

7. Jacobs *The Death and Life of Great American Cities*, pp. 62–3.

8. Xavier de Souza Briggs 'More *Pluribus*, Less *Unum*? The Changing Geography of Race and Opportunity', *The Geography of Opportunity: Race and Housing Choice in Metropolitan America*, ed. Xavier de Souza Briggs, Washington, D.C.: The Brookings Institution, 2005, pp. 34–5.

9. Jackson *Crabgrass Frontier*, pp. 207–8.

10. Briggs 'More *Pluribus* Less *Unum*?', pp. 24–5.

11. William Julius Wilson *The Truly Disadvantaged: The Inner City, The Underclass, and Public Policy,* Chicago: University of Chicago Press, 1987, pp. 4–12.

12. There is an extensive literature concerning what humans may owe to non-humans. The animal liberation and animal rights movements include consideration for animals, both wild and domestic, although they appeal to different kinds of argument; see Peter Singer *Animal Liberation: A New Ethics for our Treatment of Animals,* New York: The New York Review, 1975; Tom Regan *The Case for Animal Rights*, updated edn, Berkeley, CA: University of California Press, 2004. Biocentric or life-centered environmental ethics insists on an extension of moral consideration and even intrinsic value to all wild living

things; see Kenneth E. Goodpaster 'On Being Morally Considerable', *Journal of Philosophy* 1978, 75.6, 308–25; Paul W. Taylor 'The Ethics of Respect for Nature', *Environmental Ethics* 1981, 3.

13. Ernest Partridge 'Future Generations', *A Companion to Environmental Philosophy*, ed. Dale Jamieson, Malden, MA: Blackwell, 2001, pp. 379, 83–4.

14. Following a thread from Norton *Searching for Sustainability,* 507–9.

15. Sugie Lee and Nancy Green Leigh 'The Role of Inner Ring Suburbs in Metropolitan Smart Growth Strategies', *Journal of Planning Literature* 2005, 19.3, 335.

16. See Adam Rome *The Bulldozer in the Countryside: Suburban Sprawl and the Rise of American Environmentalism,* Cambridge: Cambridge University Press, 2001, pp. 127–8, 49–51.

17. Thanks to Steve Vogel for pointing out, in conversation, that a place might misrepresent itself.

18. According to the most widely quoted formal definition, development is sustainable if it 'meets the needs of the present without compromising the ability of future generations to meet their own needs'. The World Commission on Environment and Development *Our Common Future,* Oxford: Oxford University Press, 1987, p. 43.

19. Even John Locke, who formalized the ideas of property that came to lie at the roots of the American system of government, held that there were some limits on property rights. At the very least, people should limit themselves to what they can actually make use of, and make sure that there is enough left for others. See John Locke *Two Treatises of Government*, Cambridge Texts in the History of Political Thought, Cambridge, Cambridge University Press, 1988, pp. 290–1.

20. For a number of good examples of this kind of process with a particular emphasis on planning for habitat conservation, see Douglas R. Porter and David A Salvesen, eds, *Collaborative Planning for Wetlands and Wildlife: Issues and Examples,* Washington, D.C.: Island Press, 1995.

5. Using the Framework

1. Gillham *The Limitless City*, p. 74.

2. 'The nation . . . is just such an unwieldy and overgrown establishment,

cluttered with furniture and tripped by its own traps, ruined by luxury and heedless expense, by want of calculation and a worthy aim, as the million households in the land; and the only cure for it as for them is a rigid economy, a stern and more Spartan simplicity of life and elevation of purpose.' Henry David Thoreau *Walden and Civil Disobedience*, New York: Penguin, 1983, p. 136.

3. Roger Fisher *et al. Getting to Yes: Negotiating Agreement Without Giving In*, 2nd edn, New York: Penguin, 1991, pp. 10–11.

4. Duany *et al. Suburban Nation*, p. 33.

5. Kirkman 'Ethics and Scale in the Built Environment', 39.

6. Montgomery County, Maryland, has a long-standing policy of inclusionary zoning, which has met with considerable success. See Department of Housing and Community Affairs (Montgomery County MD), *Summary and History of the Moderately Priced Dwelling Unit (MPDU) Program in Montgomery County, Maryland*, 22 April 2005. Available: http://www.montgomerycountymd.gov/dhctmpl. asp?url=/content/dhca/housing/housing_P/Summary_and_History. asp, 10 November 2006.

7. For an overview of the problem, see Gillham *The Limitless City*, pp. 123–32.

8. Allen and Hoekstra *Toward a Unified Ecology*, pp. 51–3.

9. Kirkman 'Ethics and Scale in the Built Environment', 47–9.

10. For an overview of the new urbanism, see Congress for the New Urbanism, *Charter of the New Urbanism*, 2001, PDF. Available: http://www.cnu.org/cnu_reports/Charter.pdf, 16 October 2005; Duany *et al. Suburban Nation*.

11. See Cliff Ellis 'The New Urbanism: Critiques and Rebuttals', *Journal of Urban Design* 2002, 7.3, 261–91.

12. James Howard Kunstler *Home From Nowhere: Remaking Our Everyday World for the 21st Century*, New York: Simon and Schuster, 1996, p. 34.

13. See Duany *et al. Suburban Nation*, p. 185; Ellis 'The New Urbanism: Critiques and Rebuttals', 280.

14. See Anthony Weston *A Practical Companion to Ethics*, 3rd edn, Oxford: Oxford University Press, 2006, Chapter 3, especially pp. 38–42.

15. This is based on a situation that arose recently in a community a few miles from where I live.

16. Regarding such so-called 'greyfield' sites, see Gillham *The Limitless City*, pp. 193–5.

6. The Limits of Ethics

1. Johnson *Moral Imagination: Implications of Cognitive Science for Ethics*, pp. 36–9.
2. Following Martha Nussbaum, who writes that 'moral knowledge' is 'seeing a complex, concrete reality in a highly lucid and richly responsive way; it is taking in what is there, with imagination and feeling'. Martha C. Nussbaum *Love's Knowledge: Essays on Philosophy and Literature,* Oxford: Oxford University Press, 1990, p. 152.
3. Margaret Urban Walker 'Moral Luck and the Virtues of Impure Agency', *Moral Luck*, ed. Daniel Statman, Albany: State University of New York Press, 1993, p. 241.
4. Margaret Urban Walker refers to this kind of responsiveness as 'lucidity', and includes it among what she calls 'the virtues of impure agency'. Walker 'Moral Luck and the Virtues of Impure Agency', p. 243.
5. Claudia Card *The Unnatural Lottery: Character and Moral Luck,* Philadelphia: Temple University Press, 1996, p. 33; Lisa Tessman 'Moral Luck in the Politics of Personal Transformation', *Social Theory & Practice* 2000, 26.3, 383.
6. Tessman 'Moral Luck in the Politics of Personal Transformation', 387; see also Thomas Nagel *Mortal Questions,* Cambridge: Cambridge University Press, 1979, p. 32.
7. Kant *Groundwork*, p. 108 (Ak.440).
8. Johnson *Moral Imagination: Implications of Cognitive Science for Ethics*, p. 9.
9. Bruno Latour 'Where Are the Missing Masses? The Sociology of a Few Mundane Artifacts', *Shaping Technology/Building Society: Studies in Sociotechnical Change*, eds Weibe E. Bijker and John Law, Cambridge, MA: MIT Press, 1992.
10. Madeleine Akrich 'The De-Scription of Technical Objects', *Shaping Technology/Building Society*, eds Weibe E. Bijker and John Law, Cambridge, MA: MIT Press, 1992, p. 222; see also Stephen Graham

'The City as Sociotechnical Process: Networked Mobilities and Urban Social Inequalities', *City* 2001, 5.3, 340.

11. Tessman 'Moral Luck in the Politics of Personal Transformation', 394.

Bibliography

Akrich, Madeleine (1992) 'The De-Scription of Technical Objects' in Weibe E. Bijker and John Law (eds) *Shaping technology/building society*, Cambridge, MA: MIT Press, 205–24.

Allen, Timothy F. H. and Thomas W. Hoekstra (1992) *Toward a Unified Ecology*, New York: Columbia University Press.

Aristotle *The Nicomachean Ethics*. Trans. H. Rackham. The Loeb Classic Library. Ed. G. P. Goold. Revised edn, Vol. XIX, Cambridge, MA and London: Harvard University Press and William Heinemann Ltd, 1934.

Baldassare, Mark (1992) 'Suburban Communities', *Annual Review of Sociology* 18, 475–94.

Baxandall, Rosalyn and Elizabeth Ewen (2000) *Picture Windows: How the Suburbs Happened*, New York: Basic Books.

Bentham, Jeremy (1996) *Introduction to the Principles of Morals and Legislation*, Oxford: Oxford University Press.

Bijker, Wiebe E. (1995) 'Sociohistorical Technology Studies' in Sheila Jasanoff *et al.* (eds) *Handbook of Science and Technology Studies*, Thousand Oaks, CA: Sage Publications, 229–56.

Botkin, Daniel B. (1990) *Discordant Harmonies: A New Ecology for the Twenty-First Century*, Oxford: Oxford University Press.

Briggs, Xavier de Souza (ed.) (2005) *The Geography of Opportunity: Race and Housing Choice in Metropolitan America*, Washington, D.C.: The Brookings Institution.

Bruegmann, Robert (2005) *Sprawl: A Compact History*, Chicago: University of Chicago Press.

Bullard, Robert D., Glenn S. Johnson and Angel O. Torres (eds) (2000) *Sprawl City: Race, Politics, and Planning in Atlanta,* Washington, D.C.: Island Press.

Burchell, Robert W. *et al.* (2002) *The Costs of Sprawl - 2000.* Transit Cooperative Research Program. Vol. 74, Washington, D.C.: National Academy Press.

Burchell, Robert W., David Listokin and Catherine C. Galley (2002) 'Smart Growth: More Than a Ghost of Urban Policy Past, Less Than a Bold New Horizon', *Housing Policy Debate* 11.4, 821–79.

Burden, Dan (1999) *Street Design Guidelines for Healthy Communities,* Sacramento, CA: Local Government Commission.

Card, Claudia (1996) *The Unnatural Lottery: Character and Moral Luck,* Philadelphia: Temple University Press.

Congress for the New Urbanism (2001) *Charter of the New Urbanism.* PDF. Available: http://www.cnu.org/cnu_reports/Charter.pdf. 16 October 2005.

Department of Housing and Community Affairs (Montgomery County, MD). *Summary and History of the Moderately Priced Dwelling Unit (MPDU) Program in Montgomery County, Maryland.* 22 April 2005. Available: http://www.montgomerycountymd.gov/dhctmpl.asp?url=/content/dhca/housing/housing_P/Summary_and_History.asp. 10 November 2006.

Downs, Anthony (1999) 'Some Realities About Sprawl and Urban Decline', *Housing Policy Debate* 10.4, 955–74.

Duany, Andres, Elizabeth Plater-Zyberk and Jeff Speck (2000) *Suburban Nation: The Rise of Sprawl and the Decline of the American Dream,* New York: North Point Press.

Ellis, Cliff (2002) 'The New Urbanism: Critiques and Rebuttals', *Journal of Urban Design* 7.3, 261–91.

Ewing, Reid *et al.* (2003) 'Relationship Between Urban Sprawl and Physical Activity, Obesity, and Morbidity', *American Journal of Health Promotion* 18.1, 47–57.

Fisher, Roger, William Ury and Bruce Patton (1991) *Getting to Yes: Negotiating Agreement Without Giving In,* 2nd edn, New York: Penguin.

Fishman, Robert (1987) *Bourgeois Utopias: The Rise and Fall of Suburbia,* New York: Basic Books.

Fox, Warwick (ed.) (2000) *Ethics and the Built Environment,* London and New York: Routledge.

Frumkin, Howard (2003) 'Healthy Places: Exploring the Evidence', *American Journal of Public Health* 93.9, 1451–6.

Galster, George *et al.* (2000) 'Wrestling Sprawl to the Ground: Defining and Measuring an Elusive Concept', *Housing Facts and Findings* 2.4.

Gans, Herbert J. (1962) 'Urbanism and Suburbanism as Ways of Life: A Re-evaluation of definitions' in Arnold M. Rose (ed.) *Human Behavior and Social Processes,* Boston: Houghton Mifflin, 625–48.

— (1967) *The Levittowners: Ways of Life and Politics in a New Suburban Community,* New York: Pantheon.

Garreau, Joel (1991) *Edge City: Life on the New Frontier,* New York: Anchor Books.

Gibson, James J. (1986) *The Ecological Approach to Visual Perception,* Hillsdale, NJ: Lawrence Erlbaum Associates.

Gillham, Oliver (2002) *The Limitless City: A Primer on the Urban Sprawl Debate,* Washington, D.C.: Island Press.

Goodpaster, Kenneth E. (1978) 'On Being Morally Considerable', *Journal of Philosophy* 75.6, 308–25.

Gordon, Peter and Harry W. Richardson (2000) *Critiquing Sprawl's Critics*. Policy Analysis. Vol. 365. Washington, D.C.: Cato Institute.

Graham, Stephen (2001) 'The City as Sociotechnical Process: Networked Mobilities and Urban Social Inequalities', *City* 5.3, 339–49.

Gunn, Alistair S (1998) 'Rethinking Communities: Environmental Ethics in an Urbanized World', *Environmental Ethics* 20, 341–60.

Hempel, Carl (1996) *The Philosophy of Natural Science,* Upper Saddle River, NJ: Prentice-Hall.

Hobbes, Thomas (1968) *Leviathan,* New York: Penguin.

Hommels, Anique (2000) 'Obduracy and Urban Sociotechnical Change: Changing Plan Hoog Catharijne', *Urban Affairs Review* 35.5, 649–76.

— (2005) 'Studying Obduracy in the City: Toward a Productive Fusion between Technology Studies and Urban Studies', *Science, Technology & Human Values* 30.3, 323–51.

Hughes, Thomas P. (1986) 'The Seamless Web: Technology, Science, Etcetera, Etcetera', *Social Studies of Science* 16.2, 281–92.

— (1987) 'The Evolution of Large Technological Systems' in Wiebe E. Bijker, Thomas P. Hughes and Trevor J. Pinch (eds) *The Social Construction of Technological Systems: New Directions in the Sociology and History of Technology,* Cambridge, MA: MIT Press, 51–82.

— (1994) 'Technological Momentum' in Merritt Roe Smith and Leo Marx (eds) *Does Technology Drive History? The Dilemma of Technological Determinism,* Cambridge, MA: MIT Press, 101–13.

Hume, David (1975) *Enquiries Concerning Human Understanding and Concerning the Principles of Morals,* eds L. A. Selby-Bigge and P. H. Nidditch, 3rd edn, Oxford: Oxford University Press, 30.

Husserl, Edmund (1970) *The Crisis of European Sciences and Transcendental Phenomenology,* trans. David Carr, Evanston, IL: Northwestern University Press.

IPCC (2007) *Climate Change 2007: Synthesis Report. Contribution of Working Groups I, II and III to the Fourth Assessment Report of the Intergovernmental Panel on Climate Change,* Geneva, Switzerland: IPCC.

Jackson, Kenneth T. (1985) *Crabgrass Frontier: The Suburbanization of the United States,* Oxford: Oxford University Press.

Jackson, Richard J. (2003) 'The Impact of the Built Environment on Health: An Emerging Field', *American Journal of Public Health* 93.9, 1382–4.

Jacobs, Jane (1992) *The Death and Life of Great American Cities,* New York: Vintage Books.

Jamieson, Dale (1984) 'The City Around Us' in Tom Regan (ed.) *Earthbound: Introductory Essays in Environmental Ethics,* Prospect Heights, IL: Waveland Press, 38–73.

Johnson, Mark (1993) *Moral Imagination: Implications of Cognitive Science for Ethics,* Chicago: University of Chicago Press.

Johnson-McGrath, Julie (1997) 'Who Built the Built Environment? Artifacts, Politics, and Urban Technology', *Technology and Culture* 38.3, 690–6.

Kant, Immanuel (1958) *Groundwork of the Metaphysics of Morals,* trans. H. J. Paton, New York: Harper Torchbooks.

Kelman, Steven (1981) 'Cost-Benefit Analysis: An Ethical Critique', *Regulation* 5.1, 74–82.

King, Roger J. H. (2000) 'Environmental Ethics and the Built Environment', *Environmental Ethics* 22, 115–31.

— (2003) 'Toward an ethics of the domesticated environment', *Philosophy & Geography* 6.1, 3–14.

Kirkman, Robert (2002) *Skeptical Environmentalism: The Limits of Philosophy and Science,* Bloomington: Indiana University Press.

— (2003) 'Review of *The Skeptical Environmentalist: Measuring the Real State of the World*', *Environmental Ethics* 25, 423–6.

— (2004) 'The Ethics of Metropolitan Growth: A Framework', *Philosophy & Geography* 7.2, 201–18.

— (2004) 'Reasons to Dwell On (if Not Necessarily In) the Suburbs', *Environmental Ethics* 26.1, 77–95.

— (2004) 'Technological Momentum and the Ethics of Metropolitan Growth', *Ethics, Place and Environment* 7.3, 125–39.

— (2005) 'Ethics and Scale in the Built Environment', *Environmental Philosophy* 2, 38–52.

— (2008) 'Failures of Imagination: Stuck and Out of Luck in Metropolitan America', *Ethics, Place and Environment* 11.1, 17–32.

— (2009) 'At Home in the Seamless Web: Agency, Obduracy and the Ethics of Metropolitan Growth', *Science Technology & Human Values* 34.2, 234–58.

Kunstler, James Howard (1994) *The Geography of Nowhere: The Rise and Decline of America's Man-Made Landscape*, New York: Simon and Schuster.

— (1996) *Home From Nowhere: Remaking Our Everyday World for the 21st Century,* New York: Simon and Schuster.

Latour, Bruno (1992) 'Where Are the Missing Masses? The Sociology of a Few Mundane Artifacts' in Weibe E. Bijker and John Law (eds) *Shaping Technology/Building Society: Studies in Sociotechnical Change,* Cambridge, MA: MIT Press, 1992, 225–58.

Lee, Sugie and Nancy Green Leigh (2005) 'The Role of Inner Ring Suburbs in Metropolitan Smart Growth Strategies', *Journal of Planning Literature* 19.3, 330–46.

Leopold, Aldo (1949) *A Sand County Almanac and Sketches Here and There,* Oxford: Oxford University Press.

Light, Andrew (2001) 'The Urban Blind Spot in Environmental Ethics', *Environmental Politics* 10.1, 7–35.

Locke, John (1988) *Two Treatises of Government.* Cambridge Texts in the History of Political Thought, Cambridge: Cambridge University Press.

Lomborg, Bjørn (2001) *The Skeptical Environmentalist: Measuring the Real State of the World,* Cambridge: Cambridge University Press.

Marcuse, Peter (2000) 'The New Urbanism: The Dangers so far', *DISP* 140, 4–6.

Martinson, Tom (2000) *American Dreamscape: The Pursuit of Happiness in Postwar Suburbia*, New York: Carroll & Graf Publishers, Inc.

Marx, Leo (1964) *The Machine in the Garden: Technology and the Pastoral Ideal in America*, Oxford: Oxford University Press.

McIntosh, Robert P. (1987) 'Pluralism in Ecology', *Annual Review of Ecology and Systematics* 18, 321–41.

Merchant, Carolyn (1980) *The Death of Nature: Women, Ecology, and the Scientific Revolution*, New York: Harper and Row.

Merleau-Ponty, Maurice (1962) *Phenomenology of Perception,* trans. Colin Smith, London: Routledge.

— (1968) *The Visible and the Invisible,* trans. Alphonso Lingis, Studies in Phenomenology and Existential Philosophy, John Wild (ed.), Evanston, IL: Northwestern University Press.

Mill, John Stuart (1979) *Utilitarianism,* Indianapolis: Hackett.

Muller, Peter O. (1981) *Contemporary Suburban America,* Englewood Cliffs, NJ: Prentice-Hall.

Nagel, Thomas (1979) *Mortal Questions,* Cambridge: Cambridge University Press.

National Association of Home Builders (2000) *Smart Growth: Building Better Places to Live, Work and Play,* Washington, D.C.: National Association of Home Builders.

National Invasive Species Information Center. *European Starling.* 21 September 2006. Available: http://www.invasivespeciesinfo.gov/animals/eurostarling.shtml. 9 November 2006.

Norton, Bryan G. (2003) *Searching for Sustainability: Interdisciplinary Essays in the Philosophy of Conservation Biology*. Cambridge Studies in Philosophy and Biology, Michael Ruse (ed.), Cambridge: Cambridge University Press.

Nussbaum, Martha C. (1990) *Love's Knowledge: Essays on Philosophy and Literature,* Oxford: Oxford University Press.

Palen, J. John (1995) *The Suburbs,* New York: McGraw-Hill.

Pardales, Michael J. (2002) '"So, How Did You Arrive at that Decision?" Connecting Moral Imagination and Moral Judgment', *Journal of Moral Education* 31, 423–37.

Partridge, Ernest (2001) 'Future Generations' in Dale Jamieson (ed.). *A Companion to Environmental Philosophy*, Malden, MA: Blackwell, 377–89.

Plato 'Republic', trans. Paul Shorey, *The Collected Dialogues of Plato,* Edith Hamilton and Huntington Cairns (eds), Princeton, NJ: Princeton University Press, 1961.

Porter, Douglas R. and David A. Salvesen (eds) (1995) *Collaborative Planning for Wetlands and Wildlife: Issues and Examples*, Washington, D.C.: Island Press.

Putnam, Robert D. (2000) *Bowling Alone: The Collapse and Revival of American Community*, New York: Simon and Schuster.

Rachels, James (2003) *The Elements of Moral Philosophy,* 4th edn, Boston: McGraw-Hill.

Rawls, John (2001) *Justice as Fairness: A Restatement*, Cambridge, MA: Harvard/Belknap.

Real Estate Research Corporation (1974) *The Costs of Sprawl,* Washington, D.C.: U.S. Government Printing Office.

Regan, Tom (2004) *The Case for Animal Rights*, updated edn, Berkeley, CA: University of California Press.

Riverside Improvement Company (1871) *Riverside in 1871: With a Description of its Improvements, Together with some Engravings of Views and Buildings*, Chicago: D. & C. H. Blakely.

Rome, Adam (2001) *The Bulldozer in the Countryside: Suburban Sprawl and the Rise of American Environmentalism,* Cambridge: Cambridge University Press.

Rousseau, Jean-Jacques (1997) *The Social Contract and other Later Political Writings,* trans. Victor Gourevitch. Cambridge Texts in the History of Political Thought, Raymond Guess and Quentin Skinner (eds), Cambridge: Cambridge University Press.

Shaw, Jane and Ronald D. Utt (2000) *A Guide to Smart Growth: Shattering Myths, Providing Solutions*, Washington, D.C. and Bozeman, Montana: The Heritage Foundation and the Political Economy Research Center.

Sheehan, Molly O'Meara (2001) *City Limits: Putting the Brakes on Sprawl.* Worldwatch Paper Vol. 156, Washington, D.C.: Worldwatch Institute.

Shrader-Frechette, K. S. and E. D. McCoy (1993) *Method in Ecology: Strategies for Conservation,* Cambridge: Cambridge University Press.

Sierra Club (2000) *Smart Choices or Sprawling Growth: A 50-State Survey of Development*, San Francisco: Sierra Club.

Sies, Mary Corbin (1987) 'The City Transformed: Nature, Technology, and the Suburban Ideal, 1877-1917', *Journal of Urban History* 14.1, 81–111.

Simmons, Tavia and Grace O'Neill (2001) 'Households and Families: 2000', Washington, D.C.: U.S. Census Bureau, 8.

Singer, Peter (1975) *Animal Liberation: A New Ethics for our Treatment of Animals,* New York: The New York Review.

Starr, Chauncey (1969) 'Social Benefit Versus Technological Risk', *Science* 165.3899, 1232–8.

Stern, Robert A. M. (1986) *Pride of Place: Building the American Dream,* Boston, MA and New York: Houghton Mifflin and American Heritage.

Stilgoe, John R. (1988) *Borderland: Origins of the American Suburb, 1820-1939,* New Haven: Yale University Press.

Taylor, Paul W. (1981) 'The Ethics of Respect for Nature', *Environmental Ethics* 3, 197–218.

Tessman, Lisa (2000) 'Moral Luck in the Politics of Personal Transformation', *Social Theory & Practice* 26.3, 375–95.

The World Commission on Environment and Development (1987) *Our Common Future,* Oxford: Oxford University Press.

Thoreau, Henry David (1980) *The Natural History Essays,* Salt Lake City: Peregrine Smith.

— (1983) *Walden and Civil Disobedience,* New York: Penguin.

U.S. Department of Housing and Urban Development and U.S. Department of Commerce, 'American Housing Survey for the United States: 2007', Washington, D.C., 2008.

Walker, Margaret Urban (1993) 'Moral Luck and the Virtues of Impure Agency' in Daniel Statman (ed.) *Moral Luck,* Albany: State University of New York Press, 235–50.

Warner, Sam Bass (1978) *Streetcar Suburbs: The Process of Growth in Boston (1870-1900),* 2nd edn, Cambridge, MA: Harvard University Press.

Werhane, Patricia Hogue (1999) *Moral imagination and management decision-making,* New York: Oxford University Press.

Weston, Anthony (2001) *A 21st Century Ethical Toolbox,* Oxford: Oxford University Press.

— (2006) *A Practical Companion to Ethics,* 3rd edn, Oxford: Oxford University Press.

Wilson, William Julius (1987) *The Truly Disadvantaged: The Inner City, The Underclass, and Public Policy,* Chicago: University of Chicago Press.

Index